NEW REVISED EDITION

"...Indeed there is in the body a piece of flesh which if it is sound then the whole body is sound, and if it is corrupt then the whole body is corrupt. Indeed it is the heart."

Reported by al-Bukhārī [Eng. Trans. 1/44/no.49] & Muslim [Eng. Trans. 3/840/no.3882].

أمراض القلوب وشفاؤها

DISEASES OF THE HEARTS & THEIR CURES

by Shaykhul-Islām Ibn Taymiyyah

Translated from the original Arabic by
Abū Rumaysah

دار السنة

Daar us-Sunnah Publishers

Title
Diseases of the hearts and their cures

by
Shaykh al-Islām ibn Taymiyyah (d. 728H)

Translated from the original Arabic by
Abū Rumaysah

All inquiries must be addressed to:

دار السنة
DAAR US-SUNNAH PUBLISHERS
P.O. Box 9818
Birmingham
B11 4WA
United Kingdom
E-mail: Daar-us-Sunnah@mail.com
Website: www.daarussunnah.com
T: +44 0 121 766 7993
F: +44 0 121 766 7982

British Library Cataloguing in publication Data.
A catalogue record for this book is available from the British Library.

ISBN 1-904336-09-4
Paper-back

Published by: Daar us-Sunnah Publishers
Typeset by: Daar us-Sunnah Publishers
Cover design by: Abū Yahya
First Edition, 1419 AH/1998 CE
Second Edition, 1421 AH/2000 CE
Revised Third Edition, 1423 AH/2003 CE

Contents

CHAPTER I

Concerning the Ailments of the Hearts and their Cures.....43

CHAPTER II

Envy is a Sickness of the Heart.....85

CHAPTER III

The Disease of Desires and Passionate Love.....117

Transliteration Table

Consonants. Arabic

initial: unexpressed medial and final:

ء ʾ	د d	ض ḍ	ك k
ب b	ذ dh	ط ṭ	ل l
ت t	ر r	ظ ẓ	م m
ث th	ز z	ع ʿ	ن n
ج j	س s	غ gh	هـ h
ح ḥ	ش sh	ف f	و w
خ kh	ص ṣ	ق q	ي y

Vowels, diphthongs, etc.

Short:	ـَ a	ـِ i	ـُ u
long:	ـَا ā	ـُو ū	ـِي ī
diphthongs:		ـَوْ aw	
		ـَيْ ay	

BIOGRAPHY

Ibn Taymiyyah

May Allāh have mercy upon him

He is Aḥmad bin ʿAbdu-l-Ḥalīm bin ʿAbdu-s-Salām bin ʿAbdullāh bin Abū Qāsim ibn Taymiyyah al-Ḥarrānī Taqī ad-Dīn Abū al-ʿAbbās bin Shihāb ad-Dīn. He was born in Ḥarrān, an old city within the Arabian Peninsula between Syria[1] and Iraq, on the tenth or the twelfth of the month *Rabīʿu-l-Awwal* in the year 661H. He and his family were later forced to flee to Damascus due to the occupation by the Tartars.

He came from a family of scholars, his father and grandfather were both scholars as were three of his brothers: ʿAbdu-r-Raḥmān, ʿAbdullāh and his half-brother, Muḥammad.

During his early studies of Islām, he never ceased to amaze his teachers at the strength of his memory, keen intelligence and depth of understanding. It is said that he was first allowed to give legal verdicts at the age of nineteen and he began teaching at *Dār al-Ḥadīth as-Sukriyyah* at the age of twenty-two.

He became famous for his knowledge of ḥadīth, indeed he

---

[1] Ar. *Shām*, in those days represented the areas of Syria, Jordan and Palestine.

was a *Ḥāfidh* (Ḥadīth Master), and for his knowledge of the Qur'ān and its related sciences, he impressed all with his circles on *tafsīr*. He also attained expertise in *Usūl al-Fiqh* and *Fiqh*, knowledge of the differences of opinions present amongst the scholars, writing, mathematics, history, astronomy and medicine. Many of the scholars of his time testified that he had attained the rank of *Mujtahid*.

He always showed a great concern for the affairs and welfare of the Muslims and this manifested itself greatly in his efforts during the *Jihād* against the Tartars, Christians and *Rawāfiḍah* wherein his displays of bravery, courage and inspiring talks were one of the most important factors in the Muslims victory against their enemies. These efforts won the praise and admiration of many scholars and indeed the ensuing generations of Muslims to this very day.

Aside from the physical *Jihād*, ibn Taymiyyah launched an intellectual struggle against the various deviant sects and heretical ideas of his day. He refuted the *Shīʿa*, the People of Theological Rhetoric (*Ahl al-Kalām*) - such as the *Jahmiyyah*, *Muʿtazilah* and many of *Ashāʿirah*, the philosophers who promoted the school of the early Greeks (*falāsifa*), the majority of *Sūfi* sects and paths and the adherents of other religions. His criticisms were not based on a lack of understanding, rather he first gained an in-depth knowledge of each of these schools and as such his critique of them was systematic, acute and valid. For example it is said that his refutation of Greek philosophy was one of the most devastating attacks ever leveled against them. His refutation of Christianity was outstanding and his rebuttal of the *Shīʿa* completely demolished their beliefs and innovations from root to branch.[2]

Needless to say, these refutations, and his very direct methods of refuting, made him many enemies and as a result his life was full of trials and persecutions. His enemies were careful to look for anything by which they could attack him and they eventually found what they were looking for in his works of belief entitled *'Aqīdah al-Wāsiṭiyyah* and *'Aqīdah al-Ḥamawiyyah*. Due to their total misunderstanding of what he wrote, they accused him of anthropomorphism and had him imprisoned on more than one occasion. Ibn Kathīr mentions that some scholars sat with ibn Taymiyyah to debate with him concerning his *'Aqīdah al-Wāsiṭiyyah* and the debate ending with their agreeing with him in what he had written.[3] Similarly ibn Kathīr mentions that some scholars debated with him concerning *'Aqīdah al-Ḥamawiyyah* and his replies to their accusations could not be rebutted.[4] Ibn Taymiyyah was again imprisoned because of a legal ruling he gave concerning divorce, and yet again he was later imprisoned for a legal verdict he issued prohibiting making journeys for the purpose of visiting graves. It was during this imprisonment that he passed away.

With regards his personality and worship, he exerted a huge and lasting influence on all who met him and he was known for

---

[2] When this is understood, the critique levelled against him by some that 'his learning exceeded his intellect' can safely be relegated to the trash bin.

[3] Ibn Kathīr, *Bidāyah wa an-Nihāyah* [Vol. 14, under the heading *'Aqd Majālis ath-Thalātha*].

[4] Ibn Kathīr [14/5].

his worship and glorification of the Islāmic laws, both inwardly and outwardly. His complete reliance upon Allāh can be best summed up in what his student, ibn al-Qayyim, relates from him when he was told that his enemies had plotted to kill him or imprison him,

> If they kill me it will be martyrdom for me. If they expel me, it will be migration for me; if they expel me to Cyprus, I will call its people to Allāh so that they answer me. If they imprison me, it will be a place of worship for me.[5]

Ibn al-Qayyim himself said,

> Allāh knows, I have never seen anyone who had a better life than his. Despite the difficulties and all that expunges comfort and luxury, nay, things completely opposite to them; despite imprisonment, intimidation and oppression, ibn Taymiyyah had a purer life than anyone could. He was the most generous, the strongest of heart and the most joyful of souls, with the radiance of bliss in his face. When we were seized with fear and our thoughts turned negative, and the earth grew narrow for us, we would go to him. No sooner did we look at him and hear his words, all these feelings would leave us to be replaced by relief, strength, certainty and tranquillity.[6]

---

[5] *Nāhiyah min Ḥayāh Shaykh al-Islām* [p. 30].

[6] Ibn al-Qayyim, *Al-Wābil as-Ṣayyib* [p. 69].

Al-Bazzār said,

> I was of those who knew well his habits, he would not talk to anyone unnecessarily after the prayer of Fajr and would remain performing the *dhikr* of Allāh in a low voice which perhaps could just be heard by one sitting next to him; and frequently would he direct his gaze to the sky. This he would do until the Sun had risen high and the time in which it is prohibited to pray was over.[7]

He also said,

> I have not seen him mention any of the pleasures and attractions of this world, he did not delve into worldly conversations and he never asked for any of its livelihood. Instead he directed his attentions and conversations to seeking the Hereafter and what could get him closer to Allāh.[8]

Once, the ruler Muḥammad bin Qalāwūn accused him of wanting to wrench kingship from him due to his large following to which he replied,

> I would do that! By Allāh, your kingship and the kingship of Moghul is not even worth two meagre coins in my eyes![9]

---

[7] al-Bazzār, *al-A'lām al-'Aliyyah* [p. 40]

[8] al-Bazzār [p.52].

[9] al-Bazzār [p. 74].

His Teachers[10]

He studied under a great number of scholars and he himself mentioned a number of them as related by adh-Dhahabī directly from him.[11] This particular chronicle of teachers includes forty-one male scholars and four female scholars. The total number of scholars whom he took knowledge from exceeds two hundred.[12]

The following is a selection of some of his teachers:

- Abū al-ʿAbbās Aḥmad ibn ʿAbdu-l-Dā'im al-Maqdasī
- Abū Naṣr ʿAbdu-l-ʿAzīz ibn ʿAbdu-l-Munʿim
- Abū Muḥammad Ismāʿīl ibn Ibrāhīm at-Tanūkhī
- Al-Manjā ibn ʿUthmān at-Tanūkhī ad-Dimashqī
- Abu al-ʿAbbās al-Muʿammil ibn Muḥammad al-Bālisī
- Abū ʿAbdullāh Muḥammad ibn Abū Bakr ibn Sulaymān al-Āmirī
- Abū al-Faraj ʿAbdur-Raḥmān ibn Sulaymān al-Baghdādī
- Sharaf ad-Dīn al-Maqdasī, Aḥmad ibn Aḥmad ash-Shāfiʿī
- Muḥammad ibn ʿAbdu-l-Qawī al-Maqdasī
- Taqī ad-Dīn al-Wāsiṭī, Ibrāhīm ibn ʿAlī as-Ṣāliḥī al-Ḥanbalī
- His paternal aunt, Sitt ad-Dār bint ʿAbdu-s-Salām ibn Taymiyyah

---

[10] Refer to: *Majmūʿ Fatāwā Shaykh al-Islām* [18/76-121]; *Dhayl ibn Rajab* [2/387]; Ibn Kathīr [14/136-137]; adh-Dhahabī, *Tadhkirah al-Ḥuffādh* [3/1496]; Ibn Ḥajr al-ʿAsqalānī, *ad-Durar al-Kāminah fī Aʿyān al-Mi'ah ath-Thāminah* [1/154].

[11] *Majmūʿ al-Fatāwā* [18/76-121].

[12] *Al-ʿUqūd ad-Durriyyah* [p. 3]; *al-Kawākib ad-Durriyyah* [p. 52].

His Students

He had many students and those who were affected by him are many, some of his students were:

- Ibn al-Qayyim al-Jawziyyah, Muḥammad ibn Abū Bakr.
- Adh-Dhahabī, Muḥammad ibn Aḥmad.
- Al-Mizzī, Yūsuf ibn ʻAbdur-Raḥmān.
- Ibn Kathīr, Ismāʻīl ibn ʻUmar.
- Ibn ʻAbdu-l-Hādī, Muḥammad ibn Aḥmad.
- Al-Bazzār, ʻUmar ibn ʻAlī.
- Ibn Qāḍī al-Jabal, Aḥmad ibn Ḥusain.
- Ibn Faḍlillāh al-Amrī, Aḥmad ibn Yaḥyā.
- Muḥammad ibn al-Manj, ibn ʻUthmān at-Tanūkhī.
- Yūsuf ibn ʻAbdu-l-Maḥmūd ibn ʻAbdu-s-Salām al-Battī.
- Ibn al-Wardī, Zayn ad-Dīn ʻUmar.
- ʻUmar al-Ḥarrānī, Zayn ad-Dīn Abū Ḥafs.
- Ibn Mufliḥ, Shams ad-Dīn Abū ʻAbdullāh.

The Praise of the Scholars for him

Many scholars praised ibn Taymiyyah, not only for his scholarly achievements but also for his active participation in *Jihād* and the affairs relating to public welfare, his abundant concern for others and his worship. Below is a selection of some of these statements:

1. *Al-Ḥāfidh* adh-Dhahabī said,

> It was amazing when he mentioned an issue over which there was a difference of opinion and when he gave evidence and decided the strongest opinion - he could perform *ijtihād* due to his fulfilling its con-

ditions. I have not seen one who was quicker than he at recalling a verse which pertained to the issue that he derived from it, nor a man who was stronger in recalling texts and referring them to their sources. The *Sunnah* was in front of his eyes and upon the tip of his tongue with eloquent phrases and an open eye.

He was a sign from the signs of Allāh in *tafsīr* and expounding upon it. With regards to the foundation of the religion and knowledge of the differing opinions [on an issue], he was unequalled - this alongside his generosity, courage and lack of attention to the joys of the soul.

Quite possibly his legal rulings in the various sciences reached three hundred volumes, indeed more and he was always saying the truth for the sake of Allāh, not caring for the blame that came to him.

Whosoever associates with him and knows him well accuses me of falling short with regards to him. Whosoever opposes him and differs with him accuses me of exaggeration, and I have been wronged by both parties - his companions and his opponents.

He was white skinned with black hair and a black beard with a few grey hairs. His hair reached his earlobes and his eyes were eloquent tongues. He had broad shoulders and a loud, clear voice with a fast recitation. He was quick to anger but overcame it with patience and forbearance.

I have not seen his like for supplications [to Allāh],

his seeking succour with Him and his abundant concern for others. However I do not believe him to be infallible, rather I differ with him on both fundamental and subsidiary matters, for he - despite his vast learning, extreme courage, fluid mind and regard for the sanctity of the religion - was a man from amongst men. He could be overcome with sharpness and anger in discussion, and attack his opponents [verbally] hence planting enmity in their souls towards him.

If only he were gentle to his opponents then there would have been a word of agreement over him - for indeed their great scholars bowed to his learning, acknowledged his ability, lack of mistakes and conceded that he was an ocean having no limits and a treasure having no equivalent...

He used to preserve the prayers and fasts, glorifying the laws outwardly and inwardly. He did not give legal rulings out of poor understanding for he was extremely intelligent, nor out of lack of knowledge for he was an overflowing ocean. Neither did he play with the religion but derived evidence from the Qur'ān, *Sunnah* and *Qiyās* (analogy), he proved [his stances] and argued following the footsteps of the *Imāms* who preceded him, so he has a reward if he erred and two rewards if he was correct.

He fell ill in the castle [wherein he was imprisoned] with a serious disease until he died on the night of Monday 20th *Dhū-l-Qa'dah*, and they prayed over him in the *Masjid* of Damascus. Afterwards many talked about the number that attended his funeral prayer, and the least number given was fifty thousand.[13]

2. Ibn Ḥajr al-ʿAsqalānī said,

> The *Shaykh* of our *Shaykhs*, *al-Ḥāfidh* Abū al-Yuʿmarī [ibn Sayyid an-Nās] said in his biography of ibn Taymiyyah, 'al-Mizzī encouraged me to express my opinion on *Shaykh al-Islām* Taqī ad-Dīn. I found him to be from those who had acquired a fortune of knowledge in the sciences that he had. He used to completely memorise and implement the *Sunan* and *Āthār* (narrations). Should he speak about *tafsīr*, he would carry its flag, and should he pass a legal ruling in *fiqh*, he knew its limits. Should he speak about a ḥadīth, he was the seat of its knowledge and fully cognisant of its narrations. Should he give a lecture on religions and sects, none was seen who was more comprehensive or meticulous than he. He surpassed his contemporaries in every science, you would not see one like him and his own eye did not see one like himself...' [14]

3. Ibn Ḥajr also said,

> The acclaim of Taqī ad-Dīn is more renown than that of the sun and titling him *Shaykh al-Islām* of his era remains until our time upon the virtuous tongues. It will continue tomorrow just as it was yesterday. No one refutes this but a person who is ignorant of his prestige or one who turns away from justice...

[13] Ibn Ḥajr, [under the biography of ibn Taymiyyah].

[14] Ibid.

'Those of his stances that were rejected from him were not said by him due to mere whims and desires and neither did he obstinately and deliberately persist in them after the evidence was established against him. Here are his works overflowing with refutations of those who held to *tajsīm* (anthropomorphism), yet despite this he is a man who makes mistakes and is also correct. So that which he is correct in - and that is the majority - is to be benefited from and Allāh's Mercy should be sought for him due to it, and that which he is incorrect in should not be blindly followed. Indeed he is excused for his mistakes because he is one of the *Imāms* of his time and it has been testified that he fulfilled the conditions of *ijtihād*...

From the astonishing qualities of this man was that he was the severest of people against the People of Innovation, the *Rawāfiḍah*, the *Ḥulūliyyah* and the *Ittiḥādiyyah*. His works on this are many and famous and his *fatāwā* on them cannot be counted, so how the eyes of these innovators must have found joy when they heard those who declared him to be a *kāfir*! And how delighted they must have been when they saw those who did not declare him to be a *kāfir* in turn being labeled *kāfir*! It is obligatory upon the one who has donned the robe of knowledge and possesses intelligence that he consider the words of a man based upon his well-known books or from the tongues of those who are trusted to accurately convey his words. Then he should isolate from all of this what is rejected and warn against it with the intention of giving sincere advice and to praise him for his excellent qualities and for what he was cor-

> rect in, as is the way of the scholars.
>
> If there were no virtues of *Shaykh* Taqī ad-Dīn except for his famous student *Shaykh* Shams ad-Dīn ibn al-Qayyim al-Jawziyyah, writer of many works, from which both his opponents and supporters benefited, then this would be a sufficient indication of his [ibn Taymiyyah's] great position. And how could it be otherwise when the Shāfi'ī *Imāms* and others, not to speak of the Ḥanbalīs, of his time testified to his prominence in the [Islāmic] sciences...[15]

4. Ibn Kathīr said,

> The least he would do when he heard something was to memorise it and then busy himself with learning it. He was intelligent and had much committed to memory, he became an *Imām* in *tafsīr* and everything linked to it and knowledgeable in *fiqh*. Indeed it was said that he was more knowledgeable of the *fiqh* of the *madhhabs* than the followers of those very same *madhhabs* in his time and other than his time. He was a scholar in *Usūl* and the branches of the religion, in grammar, the language and other textual and intellectual sciences.... no scholar of a science would speak to him except that he thought that that science was the specialty of ibn Taymiyyah. As for ḥadīth then he was the carrier of its flag, a *Ḥāfidh*, able to distinguish the weak from the strong, fully acquainted with the narrators....[16]

---

[15] From Ibn Ḥajr's endorsement of *Radd al-Wāfir* contained at the end of the book.

[16] Ibn Kathīr, [14/118-119].

He also said,

> He was, may Allāh have mercy upon him, from the greatest of scholars but also from those who err and are correct. However his errors with respect to his correct rulings were like a drop in a huge ocean and they are forgiven him as is authentically reported by Bukhārī,
>
> "When a ruler makes a ruling, and he is correct then he has two rewards, and if he has erred then he has one reward."

5. *Al-Ḥāfidh* al-Mizzī said,

> I have not seen the likes of him and his own eye had not seen the likes of himself. I have not seen one who was more knowledgeable than he of the Book and the Sunnah of His Messenger, nor one who followed them more closely.[17]

6. *Al-Ḥāfidh* ʿAbdur-Raḥmān ibn Rajab al-Ḥanbalī said,

> He is the *Imām*, the legal Jurist, the *Mujtahid*, the Scholar of Ḥadīth, the *Ḥāfidh*, the Explainer of the Qurʾān, the Ascetic, Taqī ad-Dīn Abū al-ʿAbbās *Shaykh al-Islām*, the most knowledgeable of the knowledgeable. It is not possible to exaggerate his renown when he is mentioned and his fame does not require us to write a lengthy tract on him. He, may Allāh have mercy upon him, was unique in his time with respect to understanding the Qurʾān and

[17] Bahjatul Baiṭār, *Ḥayāt Shaykh al-Islām ibn Taymiyyah* [p. 21].

knowledge of the realities of faith....[18]

His Sayings

Shaykh al-Islām was famous for stating profound statements, below is a selection of some of them.

- Every punishment from Him is pure justice and every blessing from Him is pure grace.[19]

- Whoever desires everlasting bliss, let him adhere firmly to the threshold of servitude[20]

- The Lord loves to be loved.[21]

- Guidance is not attained except with knowledge and correct direction is not attained except with patience.[22]

- In this world there is a paradise, whoever does not enter it will not enter the Paradise of the Hereafter.[23]

- The one who is [truly] imprisoned is the one whose heart

---

[18] ibn Rajab, [2/387-392].

[19] *Majmū' Fatāwā* [10/85]

[20] ibn al-Qayyim, *Madārij* [1/531]

[21] *Majmū' Fatāwā* [1/54]

[22] *Majmū' Fatāwā* [10/40]

[23] ibn al-Qayyim, *al-Wābil* [p. 69]

is imprisoned from Allāh and the captivated one is the one whose desires have enslaved him.[24]

- This whole religion revolves around knowing the truth and acting by it, and action must be accompanied by patience.[25]

- Worship is founded upon the Legal Law and following it, not upon ones base desires and innovation.[26]

- If you do not taste the sweetness of an action in your heart, suspect it, for the Lord, Exalted is He, is the Appreciative.[27]

- The more the servant loves his Master, the less will he love other objects and they will decrease in number. The less the servant loves his Master, the more will he love other objects and they will increase in number.[28]

- Perpetually is the servant either the recipient of a blessing from Allāh, in which case he is need of gratitude; or he is the perpetrator of a sin, in which case he is in need of repentance; he is always moving from one blessing to

[24] Ibn al-Qayyim, *al-Wābil* [p. 69].

[25] *Majmūʿ Fatāwā* [10/38]

[26] *Majmūʿ Fatāwā* [1/80]

[27] ibn al-Qayyim, *al-Madārij* [2/68]

[28] *Majmūʿ Fatāwā* [1/94]

another and is always in need of repentance.[29]

- Sins cause harm and repentance removes the cause.[30]

- Bearing witness to *tawḥīd* opens the door of good and repentance from sins closes the door of evil.[31]

- The *Jihād* against the soul is the foundation for the *Jihād* against the disbelievers and hypocrites.[32]

- A man will never fear something besides Allāh unless it be due to a disease in his heart.[33]

- Trials and tribulation are like feeling the heat and cold, when one knows that they cannot be avoided, he will not feel anger at their onset, nor will he be distressed or disheartened.[34]

- The perfection of *tawḥīd* is found when there remains nothing in the heart except Allāh, the servant is left loving those He loves and what He loves, hating those He hates

[29] *Majmūʿ Fatāwā* [10/88]

[30] *Majmūʿ Fatāwā* [10/255]

[31] *Majmūʿ Fatāwā* [10/256]

[32] ibn al-Qayyim, *ar-Rawḍah* [p. 478]

[33] al-Bazzār [p. 74]

[34] ibn al-Qayyim, *al-Madārij* [3/289]

and what He hates, showing allegiance to those He has allegiance to, showing enmity to those He shows enmity towards, ordering what He orders and prohibiting what He prohibits.[35]

- In this world, man finds in the remembrance of Allāh, praising Him and worshipping Him, a delight that is incomparable to anything else.[36]

- The objective of asceticism is to leave all that harms the servants Hereafter and the objective of worship is to do all that will benefit his Hereafter.[37]

- Sins are like chains and locks preventing their perpetrator from roaming the vast garden of *tawḥīd* and reaping the fruits of righteous actions.[38]

- What can my enemies do to me? I have in my breast both my heaven and my garden. If I travel they are with me, never leaving me. Imprisonment for me is a chance to be alone with my Lord. To be killed is martyrdom and to be exiled from my land is a spiritual journey.[39]

---

[35] ibn al-Qayyim, *al-Madārij* [3/485]

[36] *Minhāj as-Sunnah* [5/389]

[37] *Majmū' Fatāwā* [14/458]

[38] *Majmū' Fatāwā* [14/49]

[39] ibn al-Qayyim, *Wābil* [p. 69]

His Death

Ibn Taymiyyah died while imprisoned on the twentieth of *Dhū-l-Qa'dah* of the year 728H, after ultimately being banned from reading or writing. He fell sick for the few days preceding his death.

His funeral was attended by a huge congregation despite the many lies and slanders being spread about him by certain innovators of his time. Al-Bazzār says,

> Once the people had heard of his death, not a single person in Damascus who was able to attend the prayer and wanted to remained except that he appeared and was present for it. As a result, the markets in Damascus were closed and all transactions of livelihood were stopped...Governors, heads, scholars, jurists all came out. They say that none of the majority of the people failed to turn up - according to my knowledge - except three individuals; they were well known for their enmity for ibn Taymiyyah and thus, hid away from the people out of fear for their lives.[40]

Ibn Kathīr said,

> There were so many people in front of his funeral, behind it, to its right and to its left. None but Allāh could enumerate them, and then someone shouted, 'this is how the funerals of the *Imāms* of the *Sunnah* are to be!' At that the people started to cry... when the call to prayer for *Dhuhr* was proclaimed they prayed after it straight away against the usual norm. Once they fin-

[40] al-Bazzār [pp. 82-83].

ished prayer, the deputy *khaṭīb* came out - as the main *khaṭīb* was absent and in Egypt - and he led the prayer over ibn Taymiyyah... then the people poured out from everywhere and all the doors of the Mosque... and they assembled at *al-Khayl* market. [41]

His Works

Ibn Taymiyyah was a prolific writer and authored many works spanning a broad range of topics. The sum of his writings were thought to consist of hundreds of volumes and even though a large number of them have been lost, many are still available and in print. A number of his works have also been translated and below is a list of these works followed by some of his works in Arabic. [42]

The books of, or about, ibn Taymiyyah available in the English language:

1. *Ibn Taymiyyah on Public and Private Law in Islam or Public Policy in Islamic Jurisprudence* [tr. Omar A. Farrukh, Khayats, 1966]
2. *A Seventh Century Sunni Creed: The Aqida al-Wastiya of ibn Taymiya* [tr. Merlin Swartz, the Hague: Mouton, 1973]
3. *Public Duties in Islam* [tr. Muhtar Holland, The Islamic Foundation, 1402/1982]
4. *Ibn Taymiyyah's Essay on the Jinn* [tr. Abu Ameenah Bilal Philips, 1409/1989]
5. *The Concise Legacy* [tr. Farhat Abbaas, Jamʿiyyah Ihyaa

[41] Ibn Kathīr [14/138].

[42] None of the lists detailed below are meant to be exhaustive.

Minhaaj as-Sunnah, 1415/1994]

6. *Introduction to the Principles of Tafseer* [tr. Muhammad Abdul Haqq Ansari, al-Hidaayah, 1414/1993]
7. *The Friends of Allaah and the Friends of Shaytaan* [trans. Abu Rumaysah, Daar us-Sunnah, 1421/2000].
8. *Ibn Taymiyyah Against the Greek Logicians* [tr. Wal B. Hallaq, Oxford University Press, 1993]
9. *Aqeedah al-Waasitiyyah* [tr. Assad Nimar Busool, IQRA International Educational Foundation, 1994]; *Sharh Aqeedah al-Waasitiyyah* [commentary Muhammad Khalil Harras, tr. Muhammad Rafiq Khan, Dar-us-Salam Publications, 1416/1996]
10. *Fundamentals of Enjoining Good & Forbidding Evil* [tr. Abu Khalil & Muhammad al-Jibali, al-Qur'an & Sunnah Society of North America, 1997]
11. *Mukhatasar Iqtidaa as-Siraat al-Mustaqeem* [Dar-us-Salam Publications, 1416/1996]
12. *The Book of Eemaan* [compiled from the works of ibn Taymiyyah by Dr. Muhammad Nasim Yasim, al-Firdous Ltd., 1997]
13. *Diseases of the Hearts and their Cures* [tr. Abu Rumaysah, Daar us-Sunnah, 1418/1998]
14. *Ibn Taymiyyah's Letters from Prison* [tr. Abu Ammar, Message of Islam, 1419/1998]
15. *The Waasitah Between Allaah & The Creation* [tr. Abu Iyaad Amjad Rafiq, Invitation to Islaam, 1998]
16. *Al-Ubudiyyah* [tr. Nasir ud-Deen Khattaab,]; also translated as *Ibn Taymiyyah's Essay on Servitude* [tr. Abu Safwan Fareed ibn Haibatan, al-Hidaayah, 1420/1999]
17. *Kitab al-Iman: Book of Faith* [tr. Salman Hasan al-Ani, Iman Publishing House, 1999]

18. *Ibn Taimiya's Struggle Against Popular Religion: with an annotated translation of his Kitab Iqtida as-Sirat al-Mustaqim Mukhalafat Ashab al-Jahim* [Muhammad Umar Memon, the Hague: Mouton, 1976]
19. *Ibn Taymiyyah and his Projects of Reform* [Serajul Haque, Islamic Foundation of Bangladesh, 1982]
20. *Ibn Taymiyyah's Ethics* [Victor E. Makari, Scholars Press, 1983]
21. *A Muslim Theologian's Response to Christianity: Ibn Taymiyyah's al-Jawab as-Sahih* [ed. Thomas F. Michel, Caravan Books, 1985]
22. *Economic Concepts of Ibn Taymiyyah* [Abdul Azim Islahi, The Islamic Foundation, 1408/1988]
23. *The Political Thought of ibn Taymiyyah* [prof. Qamaruddin Khan, Adam Publishers & Distributers, 1992]
24. *Ibn Taymiyyah & The Islamization of Knowledge* [Taha Jabir al-Alwani, IIIT, 1994]

The available Arabic works of ibn Taymiyyah are many, from amongst them:

1. *Majmūʿ Fatāwā ibn Taymiyyah* [compiled by ʿAbdur-Raḥmān ibn Qāsim and his son, Muḥammad in thirty-seven volumes] containing many monographs and treatise that he wrote.
2. *Fatāwā al-Kubrā*, in five volumes
3. *Fatāwā al-Miṣriyyah*
4. *Al-Jawāb as-Ṣaḥīḥ li man Baddala Dīn al-Masīḥ*, in six volumes
5. *Minhāj as-Sunnah an-Nabawiyyah*, in six volumes
6. *Darr Taʿāruḍ al-ʿAql wa-n-Naql*, in twelve volumes

7. *As-Ṣārim al-Maslūl 'alā Shātim ar-Rasūl*, in three volumes
8. *Naqd at-Ta'sīs*
9. *Iqtiḍā as-Ṣirāṭ al-Mustaqīm li Mukhālafah Aṣḥāb al-Jaḥīm*, in two volumes
10. *Al-Istiqāmah*
11. *Naqd Marātib al-Ijmā'*
12. *ar-Radd 'alā al-Manṭiqiyyīn*
13. *ar-Radd 'alā al-Akhnā'ī*
14. *ar-Radd 'alā al-Bakrī*
15. *an-Nubuwwāt*
16. *Qā'idah 'Adhīmah fī-l-Farq bayn 'Ibādah Ahl al-Islām wa-l-Īmān wa 'Ibādah Ahl ash-Shirk wa-n-Nifāq*
17. *Al-Qawā'id an-Nūrāniyyah al-Fiqhiyyah*
18. *Tafsīr ibn Taymiyyah*, compiled by 'Abdu-r-Raḥmān 'Umayrī, in seven volumes.

COMPILER'S

Foreword

All praise is due to Allāh, peace and blessings be upon the Last Prophet

Know O beloved reader that it is most important to spend one's time and energy in treating the heart, and hastening to correct and purify it from sickness and all sins. This is due to the heart occupying a great and lofty position in Islām, for it is the place to which the Lord looks and the storehouse for *tawḥīd*, faith, and sincerity.

Actions are distinguished, one from the other, with respect to their excellence in the Sight of Allāh in accordance with the condition of the heart, not by their number or form, but rather due to the strength of the caller, his or her truthfulness, his or her sincerity and the extent to which he or she prefers Allāh over himself or herself. [1]

The heart forms the foundation, it is the owner of the limbs, and the limbs are its soldiers, so when the owner becomes purified its soldiers become purified, and when the owner becomes sullied then its soldiers become sullied.

Al-Ḥāfiḍh ibn Ḥajr al-ʿAsqalānī, may Allāh have mercy upon

---

[1] As stated by Ibn al-Qayyim

him and nourish us with his knowledge, said: 'The heart has been singled out for this because it is the leader of the body, and through the purification of the leader the subjects become purified, and with his corruption they become corrupted. So if you, O servant of Allāh, wish to cure your heart then it is upon you to be truthful with regards to seeking refuge with Allāh and putting your trust in Him, to pray a great deal of superogatory prayers, to perform the actions of obedience to Allāh frequently, to pray the night prayer while the people are sleeping, and to treat your heart by making it continuously stick to the remembrances and by befriending only the righteous... and to frequently recite the Qur'ān. May Allāh allow all of this to be preserved by him.'

So my brother Muslim, this is a treatise by Shaykhul-Islām Ibn Taymiyyah concerning the topic, *'Diseases of the Hearts and their Cures.'* I found it amongst his, *'Fatāwā'* and saw it to be a beautiful work, containing many benefits. So it is upon you O Muslim to hurry to distribute this amongst your beloved friends and your brothers so that perchance Allāh may correct their hearts and Allāh's aid is sought.

Ibrāhīm bin 'Abdullāh al-Ḥāzimī.

COMPILER'S INTRODUCTION

The Keys to the Life of the Heart

Ibn ul-Qayyim, may Allāh have mercy upon him, said:

> The keys to the life of the heart lie in reflecting upon the Qur'ān, being humble before Allāh in secret, and leaving sins. [1]

Allāh, the Most High, said:

كِتَٰبٌ أَنزَلْنَٰهُ إِلَيْكَ مُبَٰرَكٌ لِّيَدَّبَّرُوٓا۟ ءَايَٰتِهِۦ وَلِيَتَذَكَّرَ أُو۟لُوا۟
ٱلْأَلْبَٰبِ ﴿٢٩﴾

> **A Book which We have sent down to you, full of blessings that they may ponder over its verses, and that men of understanding may take heed.**
>
> [*Sūrah Ṣād* (38) : 29]

So Allāh informed us that He sent down this Great Qur'ān, blessed in its wording, meaning, commands, prohibitions and regulations. Amongst its blessings is that the one who recites even one word of it then he has a reward, and this reward is

---

[1] *Ḥādiyyul-Arwāḥ ilā Bilādil-Afrāḥ* [p. 45] of Ibn ul-Qayyim.

increased tenfold, as mentioned in the *ḥadīth* reported by at-Tirmidhī, and at-Tirmidhī said that it is *ḥasan ṣaḥīḥ*.[2] Also amongst its blessings is that the one who reads it and acts upon it shall not be misguided in this world, nor fall into distress and misery in the Hereafter as stated by Ibn ʿAbbās (*raḍiyAllāhu ʿanhu*) in the commentary to the verse,

فَإِمَّا يَأْتِيَنَّكُم مِّنِّي هُدًى
فَمَنِ ٱتَّبَعَ هُدَايَ فَلَا يَضِلُّ وَلَا يَشْقَىٰ ﴿١٢٣﴾

...whoever follows My guidance shall neither go astray nor fall into distress and misery.

[*Sūrah Ṭā Hā* (20):123]

Amongst its blessings is that the one who learns it and teaches it is from the best of people as occurs in the *ḥadīth* reported by al-Bukhārī,

> The best of you is the one who learns the Qur'ān and then teaches it. [3]

Amongst its blessings is that it will be an intercessor on the

---

[2] Referring to the *ḥadīth* reported by Ibn Masʿūd (*raḍiyAllāhu ʿanhu*), that the Messenger of Allāh (ﷺ) said, 'The one who recites a word of the Qur'ān shall get one reward which then is increased tenfold. I do not say that *Alif Lām Mīm* is a word, but *Alif* is a word, *Lām* is a word, and *Mīm* is a word.'

Reported in *Riyāḍ aṣ-Ṣāliḥīn* [Eng. Trans. 2/62 no. 106], *Mishkāt al-Maṣābīḥ* [Eng. Trans. 1/452], at-Tirmidhī [no. 2912] and ad-Dārimī. It is *Ṣaḥīḥ*. Refer to *aṣ-Ṣaḥīḥah* [no. 660] and the notes of Shuʿayb al-Arna'ūṭ to *Zād al-Maʿād* of Ibn al-Qayyim [1/339]. [Translator's Note]

[3] Ṣaḥīḥ al-Bukhārī [6/501 no. 545].

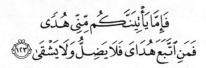

Day of Judgement for its companions who used to act by it in this world as occurs in the two *aḥādīth* reported by Muslim in his *Ṣaḥīḥ*. [4]

He, the Exalted informed us that He revealed the Qur'ān so that its meanings, commands and prohibitions may be reflected over, such that if one were to come across a verse commanding something then he should follow it. If one were to come across a verse forbidding something then he should leave it.

If one were to come across a verse concerning the Mercy of Allāh then he would hope for this Mercy and ask for it. If one were to come across a verse threatening with punishment then he would fear this and seek refuge with Allāh from it. If one were to come across a verse concerning the glorification of Allāh then he would glorify Allāh, and through this faith, knowledge, guidance and *taqwā* will increase. Allāh said while describing the

---

[4] See also the chapter, 'The Excellence of Reciting the Qur'ān' in *Riyāḍ aṣ-Ṣāliḥīn*. Referring to the *ḥadīth* of Abū Umāmah (*raḍiyAllāhu 'anhu*), that he heard the Messenger of Allāh (ﷺ) say: 'Recite the Qur'ān, for on the Day of Resurrection it will come as an intercessor for those who recite it. Recite the two bright ones, *al-Baqarah* and *Āl-'Imrān*, for on the Day of Resurrection they will come as two clouds or two shades, or two flocks of birds in ranks, pleading for those who recite them. Recite *Sūrah al-Baqarah*, for to take recourse to it is a blessing and to give it up is a cause of grief, and the magicians cannot confront it.'

And the *ḥadīth* of an-Nawwās (*raḍiyAllāhu 'anhu*), that he heard the Messenger of Allāh (ﷺ) saying: 'On the Day of Resurrection the Qur'ān and those who acted according to it will be brought with *Sūrah al-Baqarah* and *Āl-'Imrān* preceding them.' The Messenger of Allāh (ﷺ) likened them to three things, which I did not forget afterwards. 'Two clouds or two black canopies with light between them, or like two flocks of birds in ranks pleading for one who recited them.' Ṣaḥīḥ Muslim [Eng. Trans. 2/385-386 no. 1757, 1759] [Translator's Note]

believers,

وَإِذَا تُلِيَتْ عَلَيْهِمْ ءَايَٰتُهُۥ زَادَتْهُمْ إِيمَٰنًا

And when His verses are recited unto them, they increase their faith.

[*Sūrah Anfāl* (8) : 2]

Due to their containing promises and threats that motivate hope and fear; and Allāh, the Most High, said,

أَفَلَا يَتَدَبَّرُونَ ٱلْقُرْءَانَ أَمْ عَلَىٰ قُلُوبٍ أَقْفَالُهَآ ﴿٢٤﴾

Do they not ponder over the Qur'ān or are there locks upon their hearts?

[*Sūrah Muḥammad* (47) : 24]

Amongst the ways of giving life to the heart is to be humble to Allāh in secret. Meaning to desire and long for Allāh through supplication, seeking forgiveness, turning to Him, asking for victory, Paradise and shelter from Hellfire at the time when Allāh descends to the lowest Heaven in the last third of the night, as occurs in the authentic ḥadīth,

> Our Lord descends to the lowest heaven when a third of the night remains, saying: Who is supplicating to Me that I may answer him? Who is asking of Me that I may give him? Who is seeking forgiveness of Me that I may forgive him? [5]

This *ḥādīth* contains encouragement to stand in the last part of

[5] Ṣaḥīḥ al-Bukhārī [no. 9474] and Muslim [no. 758].

the night, praying, supplicating, and asking for forgiveness, Paradise and safety from the Fire, and supplicating for good in this life and the Hereafter. Indeed Allāh has commanded us with supplication and promised to reply, and He who is far removed from imperfection, does not break His promises. Amongst the times that this reply will be attained is the last part of the night, and this is a blessing that Allāh bestows upon whomsoever He wishes, and Allāh is the Possessor of great blessings and bounty. And from the ways of giving life to the heart is to leave the sins that kill it, as in the ḥadīth,

> When the servant performs a sin a black spot appears on his heart, and if he seeks forgiveness this black spot is removed, and if he returns to sin the black spot grows until his heart becomes black, and this is the *'rān'* about which Allāh spoke,
>
> كَلَّا بَلْ رَانَ عَلَىٰ قُلُوبِهِم مَّا كَانُوا يَكْسِبُونَ ﴿١٤﴾
>
> **Nay! But on their hearts is the covering of sins (*rān*) which they used to earn.**
>
> [*Sūrah ul-Muṭaffifīn* 83:14] [6]

The poet said,

'I saw the sins killing the hearts;
Breeding ignominy due to their addiction;
And in the leaving of sins lies its life;
And it is best for your soul that you preserve it.'

[6] Reported by an-Nasā'ī and at-Tirmidhī [1/128], who said it was *ḥasan ṣaḥīḥ*.

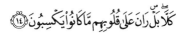

The Ailments of the Hearts and their Cures

The hearts are three types:

(i) The correct heart that is secure from all desires that oppose the command of Allāh and His prohibitions, and it is secure form all doubts that contradict what He informs. Just as it is secure from worshipping anything else besides Allah and from seeking judgement from any person other than His Messenger.

(ii) The dead heart, this being the opposite of the correct heart containing no life, neither knowing its Lord nor worshipping Him.

(iii) The heart that has some life but also has a defect. So it contains love of Allāh, faith in Him, sincerity and trust towards Him from those things that are essential to it remaining alive. It also contains the love of vain desires and preference for them, despicable morals and manners from those things that cause it to die, and it is continously wavering between these two conditions.

So the first type of heart is the living, humble, soft and gentle heart. The second is the dry, harsh and dead heart. The third is the heart which is diseased, it can either be made secure or have its destruction sealed.

All of the diseases of the heart are founded upon desires and doubts. The life of the heart and its illumination is the cause of all good to be found in it and its death and darkness is the cause of all evil to be found in it.

The heart can never be alive and correct except through cognisance of the truth, loving it and preferring it to everything else. There can never be any happiness, joy or correction for it, unless it makes its sole object of worship and desire Allāh alone.

This can never be perfected except through purification of heart, repentance, and its relinquishing itself from all types of false love and despicable manners. This can never be attained except through striving hard against one's soul that incites towards evil, and bringing it to account and combating the satans from among the jinn by holding fast to Allāh; knowing their plots and objectives, and safeguarding oneself from them through remembrance of Allāh, the Exalted, and seeking refuge with Him from them. [1]

The heart becoming defective and weak revolves around two basic matters: the corruption of knowledge and the corruption of intent. These in turn lead to two destructive illnesses - anger and misguidance. Misguidance being the end result of the corruption of intent. So these two diseases are the lords of all the ailments that afflict the heart. Its cure lies in guidance based on knowledge. Guidance based on knowledge is to know the truth and to follow it. The whole of the Qur'ān is a cure for

[1] Refer to *Ighātha al Lahfān* of Ibn al-Qayyim [1/7-10] and *Majmū' Fatāwā* of Shaykhul-Islām Ibn Taymiyyah [10/91-149].

these two diseases and others and it contains perfect guidance.[2]

[2] Refer to *Ṭarīq al-Wuṣūl ilā al-ʿIlm al-Maʿmūl bi Maʿrifah al-Qawāʿid wa aḍ-Ḍawābiṭ wa al-Uṣūl* of Ibn as-Saʿdī [p204].

Verses of the Qur'ān concerning Healing

Allāh, the Most High, said,

(i)

وَيَشْفِ صُدُورَ قَوْمٍ مُّؤْمِنِينَ ﴿١٤﴾

He will heal the breast of a believing folk.

[*Sūrah Tawbah* (9) : 14]

(ii)

وَإِذَا مَرِضْتُ فَهُوَ يَشْفِينِ ﴿٨٠﴾

And when I become sick, He heals me.

[*Sūrah Shuʿarā* (26) : 80]

(iii)

يَٰٓأَيُّهَا ٱلنَّاسُ قَدْ جَآءَتْكُم مَّوْعِظَةٌ
مِّن رَّبِّكُمْ وَشِفَآءٌ لِّمَا فِى ٱلصُّدُورِ وَهُدًى وَرَحْمَةٌ لِّلْمُؤْمِنِينَ

...There has come unto you an exhortation from your Lord, a healing for that which is in your breasts, a guidance and mercy for the believers.

[*Sūrah Yūnus* (10) : 57]

(iv)

وَنُنَزِّلُ مِنَ ٱلْقُرْءَانِ مَا هُوَ شِفَآءٌ
وَرَحْمَةٌ لِّلْمُؤْمِنِينَ وَلَا يَزِيدُ ٱلظَّٰلِمِينَ إِلَّا خَسَارًا ﴿٨٢﴾

And We reveal of the Qur'ān that which is a healing and a mercy for the believers...

[*Sūrah Isrā'* (17) : 82]

(v)

هُوَ لِلَّذِينَ ءَامَنُوا۟ هُدًى وَشِفَآءٌ

It is a guidance and a healing for those who believe.

[*Sūrah Fuṣṣilat* (41) : 44]

(vi)

يَخْرُجُ مِنۢ بُطُونِهَا شَرَابٌ مُّخْتَلِفٌ أَلْوَٰنُهُۥ فِيهِ شِفَآءٌ لِّلنَّاسِ

There comes forth from their bellies a drink of diverse hues wherein is healing for mankind.

[*Sūrah Naḥl* (16) : 69]

CHAPTER I

Concerning the Ailments of the Hearts and their Cures

Indeed all praise is due to Allāh, we seek His help, and we seek His forgiveness, and we seek refuge in Allāh from the evil of our souls and the evil of our actions. Whomsoever Allāh guides, none can misguide, and whomsoever Allāh misguides, none can guide. I bear witness that there is no deity worthy of worship except for Allāh, the One Who has no partner, and I bear witness that Muḥammad is His servant and Messenger.

Allāh the Exalted said about the hypocrites,

فِي قُلُوبِهِم مَّرَضٌ فَزَادَهُمُ ٱللَّهُ مَرَضًا

In their hearts is a disease and Allāh has increased their disease.

[*Sūrah al-Baqarah* (2) : 10]

لِّيَجْعَلَ
مَا يُلْقِي ٱلشَّيْطَٰنُ فِتْنَةً لِّلَّذِينَ فِي قُلُوبِهِم مَّرَضٌ وَٱلْقَاسِيَةِ
قُلُوبُهُمْ ۗ وَإِنَّ ٱلظَّٰلِمِينَ لَفِي شِقَاقٍ بَعِيدٍ ﴿٥٣﴾

That He may make what is thrown in by Satan

a trial for those in whose hearts is a disease and whose hearts are hardened.

[*Sūrah al-Ḥajj* (22) : 53]

لَّئِن لَّمْ يَنتَهِ ٱلْمُنَٰفِقُونَ وَٱلَّذِينَ
فِى قُلُوبِهِم مَّرَضٌ وَٱلْمُرْجِفُونَ فِى ٱلْمَدِينَةِ لَنُغْرِيَنَّكَ
بِهِمْ ثُمَّ لَا يُجَاوِرُونَكَ فِيهَآ إِلَّا قَلِيلًا ﴿٦٠﴾

If the hypocrites, and those in whose hearts is a disease, and those who spread false news among the people of Madīnah cease not, We shall certainly let you overpower them, then they will not be able to stay in it as your neighbours but for a little while.

[*Sūrah al-Aḥzāb* (33) : 60]

وَلَا يَرْتَابَ ٱلَّذِينَ أُوتُوا۟ ٱلْكِتَٰبَ وَٱلْمُؤْمِنُونَ ۙ وَلِيَقُولَ ٱلَّذِينَ فِى قُلُوبِهِم مَّرَضٌ
وَٱلْكَٰفِرُونَ مَاذَآ أَرَادَ ٱللَّهُ بِهَٰذَا مَثَلًا ۚ

...and that no doubts may be left for the People of the Book and the believers, and that those in whose hearts is a disease and the disbelievers may say, 'What does Allāh intend by this parable?'

[*Sūrah al-Muddaththir* (74) : 31]

يَٰٓأَيُّهَا ٱلنَّاسُ قَدْ جَآءَتْكُم مَّوْعِظَةٌ
مِّن رَّبِّكُمْ وَشِفَآءٌ لِّمَا فِى ٱلصُّدُورِ وَهُدًى وَرَحْمَةٌ لِّلْمُؤْمِنِينَ

...There has come to you good advice from your Lord, and a healing for that which is in the

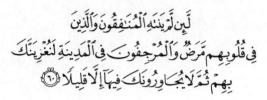

hearts, a guidance and a mercy for the believers.

[*Sūrah Yūnus* (10) : 57]

وَنُنَزِّلُ مِنَ ٱلْقُرْءَانِ مَا هُوَ شِفَآءٌ
وَرَحْمَةٌ لِّلْمُؤْمِنِينَ وَلَا يَزِيدُ ٱلظَّٰلِمِينَ إِلَّا خَسَارًا ﴿٨٢﴾

And We send down from the Qur'ān that which is a healing and mercy to those who believe, and it increases the wrong-doers in nothing but loss.

[*Sūrah al-Isrā'* (17) : 82]

وَيَشْفِ صُدُورَ قَوْمٍ مُّؤْمِنِينَ ﴿١٤﴾ وَيُذْهِبْ
غَيْظَ قُلُوبِهِمْ وَيَتُوبُ ٱللَّهُ عَلَىٰ مَن يَشَآءُ وَٱللَّهُ عَلِيمٌ حَكِيمٌ

...and heal the breast of a believing people and removes the anger of their hearts...

[*Sūrah Tawbah* (9) : 14-15]

The disease of the body is the opposite of its being sound and in good health, it is a degeneration that occurs in it causing a failure of the natural senses of perception and movement. So with respect to its perception either it goes completely such as blindness or deafness, or it perceives objects incorrectly - such as its perceiving something sweet to be bitter or its hallucinating things that have no reality in the real world. With respect to the failure of its movements then examples of this would be the inability to digest food, or the body's aversion to nourishment that it is need of, or its desire of things that would weaken it, leading to illnesses as a result of these but not leading to death or physical ruin.

Instead these failures would lead to suffering of the actual body either as a result of consuming a wrong quantity of something or applying something to the body in the wrong way. As for the first, then it could be consuming too little a quantity of nourishment and therefore the body would require more, or it could be by consuming too much and therefore the body would require it to be removed. As for the second, then it could be like extremely high or low temperatures due to incorrect usage of medicine.

The same is true for the disease of the heart for it is a type of degeneration that occurs in it, causing failure in its perception and desires. So with respect to its perception then this is degenerated by its being presented with doubts upon doubts until it cannot see the truth or it perceives the truth incorrectly. Its desires are degenerated by its hating the truth which would be of benefit to it, and loving the falsehood that would cause it harm. So this is why 'diseases' has sometimes been explained to be doubt and suspicion, as was explained by Mujāhid and Qatādah in their commentaries to the verse,

فِي قُلُوبِهِم مَّرَضٌ فَزَادَهُمُ ٱللَّهُ مَرَضًا

In their hearts is a disease and Allāh has increased their disease.

[*Sūrah al-Baqarah* (2) : 10]

and at other times to be the desire to commit fornication as in the case of the verse,

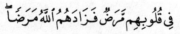

فَيَطْمَعَ ٱلَّذِى فِى قَلْبِهِۦ مَرَضٌ وَقُلْنَ قَوْلًا مَّعْرُوفًا ﴿٣٢﴾

...Lest he in whose heart is a disease be moved with desire.

[*Sūrah al-Aḥzāb* (33) : 32]

This is why al-Kharā'iṭī authored a book called, *'The book of the Weakness of the Hearts Meaning their Diseases,'* meaning by 'diseases' here - the diseases of desire.

The sick person is harmed by things that the healthy person is not, so slight heat, cold, exertion or other such things will harm him due to his inability to endure them in his weakened state. Sickness, in general, weakens the one afflicted by making his endurance weak and unable to sustain what he would have been able to sustain in a strong state. So a healthy state is preserved by remaining healthy and is removed by the opposite, and the sickness is made more severe by the presence of conditions similar to those that led to the sickness in the first place and removed by the opposite. Therefore, if a sick person is afflicted by something similar to that which led him to being sick in the first place, then he increases in illness and his endurance becomes weaker, until maybe he dies. But if he is affected by something that will increase his strength and weaken the illness then the opposite will occur.

The disease of the heart is a pain that occurs in the heart such as the anger felt towards an opponent who overcomes you, for this hurts the heart.

Allāh, the Exalted said,

وَيَشْفِ صُدُورَ قَوْمٍ مُّؤْمِنِينَ ﴿١٤﴾ وَيُذْهِبْ
غَيْظَ قُلُوبِهِمْ ۗ وَيَتُوبُ ٱللَّهُ عَلَىٰ مَن يَشَآءُ ۗ وَٱللَّهُ عَلِيمٌ حَكِيمٌ

...and heal the breast of a believing people and removes the anger of their hearts...

[*Sūrah Tawbah* (9) : 14-15]

So the healing for them was by removing the suffering that had occurred in their hearts, and it is said: 'So and so has healed his anger.' In the case of retaliation it is said: 'The close relatives of the killed sought healing,' meaning healing of their grief, anger and sorrow - all of these being sufferings that occur in oneself. Likewise doubt and ignorance cause pain to the heart. The Prophet (ﷺ) said,

> Could they not have asked if they did not know? Indeed the cure for ignorance is to ask. [1]

[1] The full text of the *ḥadīth* is narrated by Jābir bin 'Abdullāh that he said, " We went on a journey and a man from amongst us was injured in the head by a stone. After this he had a wet dream. He asked his Companions, 'Do you find that I have a concession for performing *tayammum*?' They said, 'We do not find any concession, for you are capable of employing water (for purification).' So he bathed and as a result died. When we returned to the Prophet (ﷺ) he was informed of this upon which he said, 'They have killed him, may Allāh kill them! Could they not have asked if they did not know? Indeed the cure of ignorance is to ask! It was sufficient for him to perform *tayammum*, sprinkle some water on the wound or put a bandage on his wound and then wipe over it, and wash the remainder of his body.'"

Reported in Sunan Abū Dāwūd [Eng. Trans 1/89 no. 336] and ad-Dāruquṭnī. The *ḥadīth* has a ḍa'īf sanad but it has a support from the *ḥadīth* of Ibn 'Abbās reported *Sunan Ibn Mājah* [no.572] which raises the *ḥadīth* to the level of ḥasan,

And the one who has doubt in something he has taken on board, causes harm to his heart until he attains knowledge and certainty. Hence it is said to a scholar when he answers in a way that clarifies the truth: 'you have healed me with the answer.'

[1.1 Between Sickness and Death]

Sickness is of a lesser level then death, so the heart dies due to total ignorance but becomes ill due to having fragments of ignorance, and in this case there can be either death, sickness or healing for the heart. Its life, death, sickness and the cure is greater and more vital then the life, death, sickness and cure of the body. This is why the heart becomes sick when presented with doubts and desires, or the sickness becomes more acute. If wisdom and goodly exhortation occur then theses are routes to its correction and cure.

Allāh, the Most High, says,

لِّيَجْعَلَ
مَا يُلْقِي ٱلشَّيْطَـٰنُ فِتْنَةً لِّلَّذِينَ فِي قُلُوبِهِم مَّرَضٌ وَٱلْقَاسِيَةِ
قُلُوبُهُمْ ۗ وَإِنَّ ٱلظَّـٰلِمِينَ لَفِي شِقَاقٍۭ بَعِيدٍ ﴿٥٣﴾

That He may make what is thrown in by Satan a trial for those hearts is a disease and whose hearts are hardened.

---

but the last part of the *ḥadīth* starting with 'sprinkle some water on the wound' remains ḍaʿīf. Refer to *Tamām al-Minnah* [pg. 131], *Ṣaḥīḥ Sunan Abū Dāwūd* [no. 364], *Ṣaḥīḥ Ibn Mājah* [no. 126], *Talkhīṣ al-Ḥabīr* of Ibn Ḥajr [1/260 no. 201], and *ʿAwn al-Maʿbūd* of al-Aḍhīmabādī (1/534+ along with the notes of Ibn al-Qayyim in the margin). [Translator's Note]

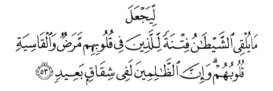

[*Sūrah al-Ḥajj* (22) : 53]

Because this breeds doubts in them and their hearts harden due to their dryness, and are weakened by doubt and become distant from faith and therefore what is thrown in by Satan becomes a trial for them.

Allāh, the Most High, said,

لَّئِن لَّمْ يَنتَهِ ٱلْمُنَٰفِقُونَ وَٱلَّذِينَ
فِى قُلُوبِهِم مَّرَضٌ وَٱلْمُرْجِفُونَ فِى ٱلْمَدِينَةِ لَنُغْرِيَنَّكَ
بِهِمْ ثُمَّ لَا يُجَاوِرُونَكَ فِيهَآ إِلَّا قَلِيلًا ﴿٦٠﴾

If the hypocrites, and those in whose hearts is a disease, and those who spread false news among the people of Madīnah cease not, We shall certainly let you overpower them, then they will not be able to stay in it as your neighbours but for a little while.

[*Sūrah al-Aḥzāb* (33) : 60]

وَلَا يَرْتَابَ ٱلَّذِينَ أُوتُوا۟ ٱلْكِتَٰبَ وَٱلْمُؤْمِنُونَ وَلِيَقُولَ ٱلَّذِينَ فِى قُلُوبِهِم مَّرَضٌ
وَٱلْكَٰفِرُونَ مَاذَآ أَرَادَ ٱللَّهُ بِهَٰذَا مَثَلًا

...and that no doubts may be left for the People of the Book and the believers, and that those in whose hearts is a disease and the disbelievers may say, 'What does Allāh intend by this parable?'

[*Sūrah al-Muddaththir* (74) : 31]

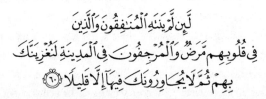

These people's heart (which have hardened) have not died as in the case of the disbelievers and the hypocrites, and neither are their hearts correct and pure like the pure hearts of the believers, rather they contains the sickness of doubt and desire. The same applies to (the ones referred to in) His saying:

فَيَطْمَعَ ٱلَّذِى فِى قَلْبِهِۦ مَرَضٌ وَقُلْنَ قَوْلًا مَّعْرُوفًا ﴿٣٢﴾

...Lest he in whose heart is a disease be moved with desire...

[*Sūrah al-Aḥzāb* (33) : 32]

Referring to the sickness of desire, for indeed if the correct heart is tempted by a woman it will not incline towards her, contrary to the heart diseased with desire, for it, due to its weakness, will incline towards what it is tempted with in accordance to the strength or the weakness of the sickness, and when it submits to the temptation, the sickness in the heart is satiated.

[1.2 The Qur'ān is a cure for the hearts]

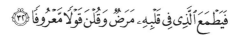

The Qur'ān is a cure for that which is within the heart, and for the one who has the sickness of doubt and desire in his heart, for it contains clear proofs that distinguish the truth from falsehood, and remove the sickness of false doubts to leave certain knowledge, correct perception and understanding such that the heart sees things in accordance to their reality. It contains wisdom, goodly exhortations both encouraging good and deterring from evil, and stories which contain lessons that necessarily lead to the correction of the heart by making the heart desire what is good for it and detest what is harmful to it. Hence the heart is left desiring that which will guide it, hating that which will deviate it after it used to desire that which would deviate it and hate that which would guide it.

The Qur'ān removes all the sicknesses that invoke false desires until the heart becomes pure and therefore its desires become pure and it returns to the natural state (*fiṭrah*) that it was created in, just as the body returns to the natural state upon being treated. The heart will be nurtured with faith and the Qur'ān such that it will become strong - for indeed the purification of the heart is like the growing of the body.

[1.3 Righteous Actions are a Cure for the Heart]

Zakāh (purification) in the language means: growth and increase in correction, it is said, 'something has *zakāh*', when it has grown in correction. The heart is in need of being nurtured so that it may mature and increase until it becomes complete and correct just as the body is in need of nourishment that is good for it, but along with this there is a need to prevent anything from harming it. So the body will not grow until it gains that which will benefit it and is prevented from that which will harm it, likewise the heart will not become pure such that it may grow and become complete with respect to its correction, until it attains that which benefits it and represses that which harms it - just as the flower will not grow without these two factors.

Ṣadaqah (charity), due to its extinguishing the sins as water extinguishes fire, causes the heart to be purified. Its *zakāh* means something additional to it being merely free of sins.

Allāh the Exalted said,

خُذْ مِنْ أَمْوَٰلِهِمْ صَدَقَةً تُطَهِّرُهُمْ وَتُزَكِّيهِم بِهَا وَصَلِّ عَلَيْهِمْ

Take *ṯadaqah* from them in order to purify them and sanctify them with it.

[*Sūrah Tawbah* (9) : 103]

[1.4 Leaving Indecent Actions are a Cure for the Heart]

Similarly abstaining from indecent actions and sins leads to purification of the heart, for these are of the same level as leprosy of the body or thorns on a flower. So when the body is freed of this leprosy by releasing the additional blood for example, the natural strength of the body emerges and it can find relief and thereby grow. Likewise when one seeks repentance from sin, the heart is released from contamination - whereby it mixed the righteous actions with evils actions, so when one repents from sins the strength of the heart emerges as does its desire to perform righteous actions and it finds relief from these false and corrupt matters that it was submerged in.

So the *zakāh* of the heart means its growing and becoming complete. Allāh the Exalted said,

وَلَوْلَا فَضْلُ
ٱللَّهِ عَلَيْكُمْ وَرَحْمَتُهُۥ مَا زَكَىٰ مِنكُم مِّنْ أَحَدٍ أَبَدًا وَلَٰكِنَّ ٱللَّهَ يُزَكِّى

And had it not been for the Grace of Allāh and His Mercy on you, not one of you would ever have been pure from sins...

[*Sūrah an-Nūr* (24) : 21]

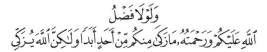

فَإِن لَّمْ تَجِدُوا فِيهَا أَحَدًا فَلَا تَدْخُلُوهَا حَتَّىٰ يُؤْذَنَ لَكُمْ وَإِن
قِيلَ لَكُمُ ارْجِعُوا فَارْجِعُوا هُوَ أَزْكَىٰ لَكُمْ وَاللَّهُ بِمَا تَعْمَلُونَ
عَلِيمٌ ﴿٢٨﴾

...And if you are asked to go back, then go back, for it is purer for you...

[*Sūrah an-Nūr* (24) : 28]

قُل لِّلْمُؤْمِنِينَ يَغُضُّوا مِنْ أَبْصَارِهِمْ وَيَحْفَظُوا فُرُوجَهُمْ
ذَٰلِكَ أَزْكَىٰ لَهُمْ إِنَّ اللَّهَ خَبِيرٌ بِمَا يَصْنَعُونَ ﴿٣٠﴾

Tell the believing men to lower their gaze and protect their private parts. That is purer for them...

[*Sūrah an-Nūr* (24) : 30]

قَدْ أَفْلَحَ مَن تَزَكَّىٰ ﴿١٤﴾ وَذَكَرَ اسْمَ رَبِّهِ فَصَلَّىٰ ﴿١٥﴾

Indeed whoever purifies himself shall achieve success, and remembers the Name of his Lord and prays.

[*Sūrah al-A'lā* (87) : 14-15]

قَدْ أَفْلَحَ مَن زَكَّاهَا ﴿٩﴾ وَقَدْ خَابَ مَن دَسَّاهَا ﴿١٠﴾

Indeed he succeeds who purifies himself, and indeed he fails who corrupts his self.

[*Sūrah ash-Shams* (91) : 9-10]

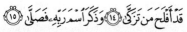

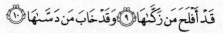

وَمَا يُدْرِيكَ لَعَلَّهُۥ يَزَّكَّىٰٓ ﴿٣﴾

But what could tell you that perchance he might become pure?

[*Sūrah ʿAbasa* (80) : 3]

فَقُلْ هَل لَّكَ إِلَىٰٓ أَن تَزَكَّىٰ ﴿١٨﴾ وَأَهْدِيَكَ إِلَىٰ رَبِّكَ فَتَخْشَىٰ ﴿١٩﴾

And say to him (i.e. Firʿaun); 'Would you purify yourself, and that I guide you to your Lord, so you should fear Him?'

[*Sūrah an-Nāziʿāt* (79) : 18-19]

So *tazkiyyah* (purification), even if its basic meaning is growth, blessing and increase in goodness, is only attained by removing the evil, and this is why purification has come to combine both these matters (i.e., performing good and avoiding evil).

He, the Most High, said,

وَوَيْلٌ لِّلْمُشْرِكِينَ ﴿٦﴾ ٱلَّذِينَ لَا يُؤْتُونَ ٱلزَّكَوٰةَ وَهُم بِٱلْـَٔاخِرَةِ هُمْ كَـٰفِرُونَ ﴿٧﴾

And woe to the polytheists, those who do not give the *zakāh*, and are disbelievers in the Hereafter.

[*Sūrah Fuṣṣilāt* (41) : 6-7]

Meaning by *zakāh*, the *tawḥīd* and *īmān* by which the heart is purified, for indeed *tawḥīd* includes negating any lordship besides Allāh and affirming the Lordship of Allāh in the heart, this being the reality of *'Lā Ilāha Illā Allāh'* (there is none worthy of worship except Allāh) and this being the basis by which the hearts are purified.

Tazkiyyah (purification) is the act of making something pure, either in and of itself, or in belief, or in reports. It is similarly said: *'adaltuhu'* when you made it just, in and of itself, or in the belief of the people.

Allāh, The Most High, said,

فَلَا تُزَكُّوٓاْ أَنفُسَكُمۡۖ

So do not ascribe purity (*tuzakkū*) to yourself...

[*Sūrah Najm* (53) : 32]

i.e. do not broadcast that you are pure, and this is not the same as His saying

قَدۡ أَفۡلَحَ مَن زَكَّىٰهَا ٩

Indeed he succeeds who purifies himself.

[*Sūrah ash-Shams* (91) : 9]

This is why Allāh, the Most High, said,

هُوَ أَعۡلَمُ بِمَنِ ٱتَّقَىٰٓ ٣٢

He knows best who fear Allāh.

[*Sūrah Najm* (53) : 32]

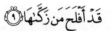

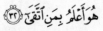

Zaynab was initially known as Burrā, and it is said that she

purified herself and so the Messenger of Allāh (ﷺ) called her Zaynab. As for the saying of Allāh,

أَلَمْ تَرَ إِلَى ٱلَّذِينَ يُزَكُّونَ أَنفُسَهُم ۚ بَلِ ٱللَّهُ يُزَكِّى مَن يَشَآءُ

Have you not seen those who claim purity for themselves, nay - but Allāh purifies (*yuzakkī*) whom He pleases.

[*Sūrah an-Nisā'* (4) : 49]

Meaning He makes pure whomsoever He pleases and makes his purity known, just as the purifier declares to be pure only those whose justice he can bear testimony to.

[1.5 The Effect of Sins Upon the Purity of the Heart]

'Adl (fairness and justice) is *I'tidāl* (balance), and in balance lies the correction of the heart, just as in *ẓulm* (imbalance/ oppression) lies its corruption. This is why for every sin that the person has committed he has oppressed his self (*ẓāliman lī nafsihi*). The opposite of *ẓulm* is *'adl*, so this sinful person has not been just to his self rather he has oppressed it. The correction of the heart lies in *'adl* and its corruption lies in *ẓulm*. Therefore, when the servant oppresses himself he is the oppressor and oppressed at the same time, likewise when he is just then he is the one who is just and the one upon whom the justice is carried out.

The person does an action and he will receive the fruit of this action, be it bitter or sweet.

Allāh said,

لَهَا مَا كَسَبَتْ وَعَلَيْهَا مَا ٱكْتَسَبَتْ

...He has the reward for the (good) that he has earned, and he is punished for the (evil) which he has earned...

[*Sūrah al-Baqarah* (2) : 286]

'Aml (actions) have an effect upon the heart, either of benefit, harm, or correction, before they effect the external body. The good and pure actions constitute justice for the soul whereas bad actions oppress the soul.

Allāh the Most High, said,

مَّنْ عَمِلَ صَٰلِحًا فَلِنَفْسِهِۦ ۖ وَمَنْ أَسَآءَ فَعَلَيْهَا ۗ وَمَا رَبُّكَ بِظَلَّٰمٍ لِّلْعَبِيدِ ﴿٤٦﴾

Whoever does righteous deeds it is for the (benefit of) himself, and whosoever does evil, it is against his own self.

[*Sūrah Fuṣṣilat* (41) : 46]

إِنْ أَحْسَنتُمْ أَحْسَنتُمْ لِأَنفُسِكُمْ ۖ وَإِنْ أَسَأْتُمْ فَلَهَا ۚ

If you do good, you do good for your own selves, and if you do evil, you do it against yourselves.

[*Sūrah al-Isrā'* (17) : 7]

Some of the *Salaf*[2] said, 'Indeed good actions are a light in the heart, a strengthening for the body, a glow on the face, a cause

[2] i.e. Ibn 'Abbās as mentioned by Ibn al-Qayyim in *al-Jawāb al-Kāfī*.

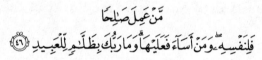

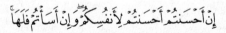

for extensive provisions and love in the hearts of the creation. Indeed bad actions are a darkness in the heart, a blackness on the face, a weakness for the body, a cause for decrease in provisions and hatred in the hearts of the creation.'

Allāh, the Most High, said,

كُلُّ ٱمْرِيٍٕۭ بِمَا كَسَبَ رَهِينٌ ﴿٢١﴾

Every person has a pledge for that which he has earned.

[*Sūrah at-Ṭūr* (52) : 21]

كُلُّ نَفْسٍۭ بِمَا كَسَبَتْ رَهِينَةٌ ﴿٣٨﴾

Every person has a pledge for what he has earned.

[*Sūrah al-Muddaththir* (74) : 38]

وَذَكِّرْ بِهِۦٓ
أَن تُبْسَلَ نَفْسٌۢ بِمَا كَسَبَتْ لَيْسَ لَهَا مِن دُونِ ٱللَّهِ وَلِيٌّ
وَلَا شَفِيعٌ وَإِن تَعْدِلْ كُلَّ عَدْلٍ لَّا يُؤْخَذْ مِنْهَآ ۗ أُوْلَٰٓئِكَ
ٱلَّذِينَ أُبْسِلُوا۟ بِمَا كَسَبُوا۟ ۖ

But remind (them) of it (the Qur'ān) lest a person be given up to destruction (*tubsala*) for that which he has earned, when he will find for himself no protector or intercessor besides Allāh. And even if he offers every ransom, it will not be accepted from him. Such are they

who are given up to destruction because of that which they earned.

[*Sūrah al-An'ām* (6) : 70]

Tubsala means: to repress, to fetter and captivate.

Similarly when the body has recovered from illness it is said: 'He has balanced his temperament and disposition.' This is because the sickness distorts the temperament, despite the fact that there is no way to achieve complete balance, safe from mixing both justice and injustice - but the ideal or close to the ideal should be aimed for.

The same case applies to the heart, its health and correction lies in balance, and its sickness lies in deviation, oppression and digression. But complete balance in everything is impossible, in action or knowledge - but the ideal or the closest to the ideal should be aimed for. This is why it is said, describing the *Salafi* way: 'the ideal way.'

Allāh said

وَلَن تَسْتَطِيعُوٓاْ أَن تَعْدِلُواْ
بَيْنَ ٱلنِّسَآءِ وَلَوْ حَرَصْتُمْ فَلَا تَمِيلُواْ كُلَّ ٱلْمَيْلِ

And you will never be able to be just between the wives, even if you desire to be...

[*Sūrah an-Nisā'* (4) : 129]

وَأَوْفُوا۟ ٱلْكَيْلَ وَٱلْمِيزَانَ بِٱلْقِسْطِ ۖ لَا نُكَلِّفُ نَفْسًا إِلَّا وُسْعَهَا ۖ

And give full measure and full weight. We do not burden a soul beyond what it can bear.

[*Sūrah al-Anʿām* (6) : 152]

Allāh, the Exalted, sent the messengers and revealed the Books so that man may establish justice, and the greatest form of justice is to worship Allāh alone with no partner; then giving due justice to the rights of man; then being just upon oneself.

[1.6 Types of *Ẓulm*]

Ẓulm is of three types, and all of these are from the sicknesses of the heart, and in justice lies its good health and purity. Imām Aḥmad bin Ḥanbal said to one of the people, 'If you were healthy you would not fear anyone,' meaning that the fear you have of men is due to a sickness from within you, such as the sickness of shirk and sins.

The basis of the heart being corrected lies in it being alive and enlightened.

Allāh, the Most High, said,

أَوَمَن كَانَ مَيْتًا فَأَحْيَيْنَٰهُ وَجَعَلْنَا لَهُۥ نُورًا يَمْشِى بِهِۦ فِى ٱلنَّاسِ كَمَن مَّثَلُهُۥ فِى ٱلظُّلُمَٰتِ لَيْسَ بِخَارِجٍ مِّنْهَا

Is he who was dead and We gave him life and set for him a light whereby he can walk amongst

men, like him who is in the darkness of disbelief from which he can never come?

[*Sūrah al-An'ām* (6) : 122]

This is why Allāh has mentioned the life of the heart, its illumination, death and darkness in a number of places, like His, the Exalted's saying,

لِّيُنذِرَ مَن كَانَ حَيًّا

That he may give warning to he who is alive

[*Sūrah Yā-Sīn* (36) : 70]

يَـٰٓأَيُّهَا ٱلَّذِينَ
ءَامَنُوا۟ ٱسْتَجِيبُوا۟ لِلَّهِ وَلِلرَّسُولِ إِذَا دَعَاكُمْ لِمَا يُحْيِيكُمْ ۖ
وَٱعْلَمُوٓا۟ أَنَّ ٱللَّهَ يَحُولُ بَيْنَ ٱلْمَرْءِ وَقَلْبِهِۦ وَأَنَّهُۥٓ إِلَيْهِ
تُحْشَرُونَ ﴿٢٤﴾

O you who believe! Answer the call of Allāh and His Messenger when he calls you to that which gives you life, and know that Allāh comes in between a person and his heart. And verily to Him you shall be gathered.

[*Sūrah al-Anfāl* (8) : 24]

يُخْرِجُ ٱلْحَىَّ مِنَ ٱلْمَيِّتِ وَيُخْرِجُ ٱلْمَيِّتَ مِنَ ٱلْحَىِّ

He brings out the living from the dead, and brings out the dead from the living

[*Sūrah ar-Rūm* (30) : 19]

From the examples of this is His bringing forth a believer from a disbeliever, and a disbeliever from a believer.

In the authentic *ḥadīth*,

> The similitude of a house in which Allāh is mentioned, and the house in which Allāh is not mentioned is as the living and the dead.[3]

In the *Ṣaḥīḥ* (of al-Bukhārī) is the *ḥadīth*,

> Perform some of your prayers in your houses, and do not take them as graves. [4]

Allāh, the Most High, has said,

وَٱلَّذِينَ كَذَّبُوا۟ بِـَٔايَٰتِنَا صُمٌّ وَبُكْمٌ فِى ٱلظُّلُمَٰتِ

Those who reject our signs are deaf, dumb and in darkness.

[*Sūrah al-An'ām* (6) : 39]

Allāh has mentioned the 'Verse of Light' and the 'Verse of Darkness' saying,

[3] *Ṣaḥīḥ al-Bukhārī* [Eng. Trans. 8/278 no. 416].

[4] *Ṣaḥīḥ al-Bukhārī* [Eng. Trans. 1/254 no. 424, 2/156 no. 280].

ٱللَّهُ نُورُ ٱلسَّمَٰوَٰتِ
وَٱلْأَرْضِ ۚ مَثَلُ نُورِهِۦ كَمِشْكَوٰةٍ فِيهَا مِصْبَاحٌ ۖ ٱلْمِصْبَاحُ فِى زُجَاجَةٍ ۖ
ٱلزُّجَاجَةُ كَأَنَّهَا كَوْكَبٌ دُرِّىٌّ يُوقَدُ مِن شَجَرَةٍ مُّبَٰرَكَةٍ زَيْتُونَةٍ
لَّا شَرْقِيَّةٍ وَلَا غَرْبِيَّةٍ يَكَادُ زَيْتُهَا يُضِىٓءُ وَلَوْ لَمْ تَمْسَسْهُ نَارٌ ۚ
نُّورٌ عَلَىٰ نُورٍ ۗ يَهْدِى ٱللَّهُ لِنُورِهِۦ

Allāh is the Light of the heavens and the earth. The parable of His Light is as (if there were) a niche and within it a lamp, the lamp is in the glass, the glass as it were a brilliant star, lit from a blessed tree, an olive neither of the east or west, whose oil would almost glow forth (of itself), though no fire touched it. Light upon Light!

[*Sūrah an-Nūr* (24) : 35]

This is the similitude for the light of faith in the hearts of the believers. Then He said,

وَٱلَّذِينَ كَفَرُوٓا۟ أَعْمَٰلُهُمْ كَسَرَابٍۭ
بِقِيعَةٍ يَحْسَبُهُ ٱلظَّمْـَٔانُ مَآءً حَتَّىٰٓ إِذَا جَآءَهُۥ لَمْ يَجِدْهُ شَيْـًٔا
وَوَجَدَ ٱللَّهَ عِندَهُۥ فَوَفَّىٰهُ حِسَابَهُۥ ۗ وَٱللَّهُ سَرِيعُ ٱلْحِسَابِ ﴿٣٩﴾
أَوْ كَظُلُمَٰتٍ فِى بَحْرٍ لُّجِّىٍّ يَغْشَىٰهُ مَوْجٌ مِّن فَوْقِهِۦ مَوْجٌ مِّن
فَوْقِهِۦ سَحَابٌ ۚ ظُلُمَٰتٌۢ بَعْضُهَا فَوْقَ بَعْضٍ إِذَآ أَخْرَجَ يَدَهُۥ لَمْ
يَكَدْ يَرَىٰهَا ۗ وَمَن لَّمْ يَجْعَلِ ٱللَّهُ لَهُۥ نُورًا فَمَا لَهُۥ مِن نُّورٍ ﴿٤٠﴾

As for those who disbelieve, their deeds are like

a mirage in a desert. The thirsty one thinks it to be water, until he comes up to it, he finds it to be nothing, but He finds Allaah with him, Who will pay his due (in Hell). And Allāh is Swift in taking account. Or (the state of the disbeliever) is like the darkness in a vast deep sea, overwhelmed with a great wave, topped by dark clouds - darkness one above another - if a man stretches out his hand, he can hardly see it! And he for whom Allāh has not appointed light, there is no light.

[*Sūrah an-Nūr* (24) : 39-40]

So the first verse (no. 39) sets forth a similitude for the false beliefs and the actions that arise from these beliefs, one considers them to be something of benefit, but when they come to him (on the day of Judgement) he will not find any benefit in them at all. Rather Allāh will fully give him his recompense for these actions (in Hell). The second verse (no. 40) is the similitude propounded for extensive ignorance, lack of faith and (correct) knowledge. The person who possesses these is in darknesses one above another, unable to see anything, for indeed the sight occurs only with the light of faith and (correct) knowledge.

Allāh, the Most High, said,

إِنَّ ٱلَّذِينَ ٱتَّقَوْاْ إِذَا مَسَّهُمْ طَٰٓئِفٌ مِّنَ ٱلشَّيْطَٰنِ تَذَكَّرُواْ
فَإِذَا هُم مُّبْصِرُونَ ﴿٢٠١﴾

Indeed, those who are pious, when an evil

thought comes to them from Satan, they remember (Allāh), and they then see (aright).

[*Sūrah al-Aʿrāf* (7) : 201]

وَلَقَدْ هَمَّتْ بِهِۦ وَهَمَّ بِهَا لَوْلَآ أَن رَّءَا بُرْهَـٰنَ رَبِّهِۦ

And indeed she did desire him and he (Yūsuf) would have inclined to her desire, had he not seen the evidence of his Lord.

[*Sūrah Yūsuf* (12) : 24]

Meaning the proof of faith which his heart had attained, so due to this Allāh caused him to turn away from that which he was inclined to, and recorded for him a complete good deed, and no sin was recorded against him due to his having performed a good action and not performed an evil one.

Allāh, the Exalted said,

الٓر ۚ كِتَـٰبٌ أَنزَلْنَـٰهُ إِلَيْكَ لِتُخْرِجَ ٱلنَّاسَ مِنَ ٱلظُّلُمَـٰتِ
إِلَى ٱلنُّورِ بِإِذْنِ رَبِّهِمْ إِلَىٰ صِرَٰطِ ٱلْعَزِيزِ ٱلْحَمِيدِ ﴿١﴾

...In order that you might lead mankind out of darkness into light...

[*Sūrah Ibrāhīm* (14) : 1]

ٱللَّهُ وَلِىُّ ٱلَّذِينَ ءَامَنُوا۟ يُخْرِجُهُم مِّنَ ٱلظُّلُمَـٰتِ إِلَى ٱلنُّورِ ۖ
وَٱلَّذِينَ كَفَرُوٓا۟ أَوْلِيَآؤُهُمُ ٱلطَّـٰغُوتُ يُخْرِجُونَهُم مِّنَ
ٱلنُّورِ إِلَى ٱلظُّلُمَـٰتِ ۗ

Allāh is the Protector of those who believe. He

brings them out from the darkness into the light. But as for those who disbelieve their protectors are false deities, they bring them out from the light into the darkness.

[*Sūrah al-Baqarah* (2) : 257]

يَـٰٓأَيُّهَا ٱلَّذِينَ ءَامَنُوا۟ ٱتَّقُوا۟ ٱللَّهَ
وَءَامِنُوا۟ بِرَسُولِهِۦ يُؤْتِكُمْ كِفْلَيْنِ مِن رَّحْمَتِهِۦ وَيَجْعَل لَّكُمْ
نُورًا تَمْشُونَ بِهِۦ وَيَغْفِرْ لَكُمْ ۚ وَٱللَّهُ غَفُورٌ رَّحِيمٌ ﴿٢٨﴾

O you who believe (in Moses and Jesus)! Fear Allāh and believe in His Messenger, He will give you a double portion of His Mercy, and He will give you a light by which you shall walk straight...

[*Sūrah al-Ḥadīd* (57) : 28]

This is why Allāh has propounded two types of parables for faith: a parable of water by which life exists and the foam which comes with it; and a parable of fire by which light is produced.

Allāh said,

أَنزَلَ مِنَ
ٱلسَّمَآءِ مَآءً فَسَالَتْ أَوْدِيَةٌۢ بِقَدَرِهَا فَٱحْتَمَلَ ٱلسَّيْلُ زَبَدًا رَّابِيًا ۚ
وَمِمَّا يُوقِدُونَ عَلَيْهِ فِى ٱلنَّارِ ٱبْتِغَآءَ حِلْيَةٍ أَوْ مَتَـٰعٍ زَبَدٌ مِّثْلُهُۥ ۚ كَذَٰلِكَ
يَضْرِبُ ٱللَّهُ ٱلْحَقَّ وَٱلْبَـٰطِلَ ۚ فَأَمَّا ٱلزَّبَدُ فَيَذْهَبُ جُفَآءً ۖ

He sends down water (rain) from the sky, and

the valleys flow according to their measure, but the floods bears away the foam that mounts up on the surface, and also from that (ore) which they heat in the fire in order to make ornaments or utensils, rises a foam like unto it, thus does Allāh (by parables) show forth truth from falsehood...

[*Sūrah ar-Ra'd* (13) : 17]

Similarly Allāh has propounded two parables for hypocrisy,

مَثَلُهُمْ كَمَثَلِ ٱلَّذِى ٱسْتَوْقَدَ نَارًا فَلَمَّآ أَضَآءَتْ مَا حَوْلَهُۥ
ذَهَبَ ٱللَّهُ بِنُورِهِمْ وَتَرَكَهُمْ فِى ظُلُمَٰتٍ لَّا يُبْصِرُونَ ﴿١٧﴾ صُمٌّۢ
بُكْمٌ عُمْىٌ فَهُمْ لَا يَرْجِعُونَ ﴿١٨﴾ أَوْ كَصَيِّبٍ مِّنَ ٱلسَّمَآءِ فِيهِ
ظُلُمَٰتٌ وَرَعْدٌ وَبَرْقٌ يَجْعَلُونَ أَصَٰبِعَهُمْ فِىٓ ءَاذَانِهِم مِّنَ ٱلصَّوَٰعِقِ
حَذَرَ ٱلْمَوْتِ ۚ وَٱللَّهُ مُحِيطٌۢ بِٱلْكَٰفِرِينَ ﴿١٩﴾ يَكَادُ ٱلْبَرْقُ يَخْطَفُ
أَبْصَٰرَهُمْ ۖ كُلَّمَآ أَضَآءَ لَهُم مَّشَوْا۟ فِيهِ وَإِذَآ أَظْلَمَ عَلَيْهِمْ قَامُوا۟ ۚ
وَلَوْ شَآءَ ٱللَّهُ لَذَهَبَ بِسَمْعِهِمْ وَأَبْصَٰرِهِمْ ۚ إِنَّ ٱللَّهَ عَلَىٰ كُلِّ
شَىْءٍ قَدِيرٌ ﴿٢٠﴾

Their likeness is as the likeness of one who kindled a fire; then, when it lighted all around him, Allāh took away their light and left them in darkness so they could not see. They are deaf, dumb and blind - so they will not return (to the Right Path). Or like a rainstorm from the sky, wherein is darkness, thunder and lightening. They thrust their fingers in their ears to keep out the stun-

> **ning thunderclap for fear of death. But Allāh ever encompasses the disbelievers. The lightening almost snatches away their sight, whenever it flashes for them they stand still. And if Allāh willed, He could have taken away their hearing and their sight. Indeed Allāh has power over all things.**
>
> [*Sūrah al-Baqarah* (2) : 17-20]

So He propounded a parable for them with one who kindled a fire, each time it ignited Allāh caused it to extinguish, and the parable of water in which the water is sent down containing darkness, thunder and lightening - this is not the place for a detailed explanation of these parables for the purpose here is only to mention the life of the heart and its illumination.

[1.7 The Life of the Heart]

In the narrated *du'ā* there occurs,

> Make the Qur'ān the nurturer (*rabī'*) of our hearts and the light of our chest. [5]

Rabī': means the rain that descends from the sky and nourishes the plants. The Arabs call the season in which the rain first descends al-Rabī' due to the fall of rain which causes growth (of produce). The non-Arabs call the season that follow winter al-Rabī' because in this season the plants from which fruit is

[5] Part of a lengthy supplication reported by Aḥmad [3712], Abū Ya'lā [q 1/156], at-Ṭabarānī in *al-Kabīr* [3/74/1] and others. The *ḥadīth* is *ṣaḥīḥ*. Refer to *aṣ-Ṣaḥīḥah* [no. 199]. The wording of this *ḥadīth* of Aḥmad, however, is in a singular gender not plural. [Translator's Note]

produced blossom and the leaves on the trees appear.

[1.8 The State of the Dead Heart]

The heart that is alive and enlightened hears, sees and understands due to the light that it contains, while the dead heart does not hear, see or understand.

Allāh, the Exalted said,

وَمَثَلُ ٱلَّذِينَ كَفَرُوا۟ كَمَثَلِ ٱلَّذِى يَنْعِقُ
بِمَا لَا يَسْمَعُ إِلَّا دُعَآءً وَنِدَآءً ۚ صُمٌّۢ بُكْمٌ عُمْىٌ فَهُمْ لَا يَعْقِلُونَ

The example of those who disbelieve, is as that of him who shouts to the (flock of sheep) that hears nothing but calls and cries. (They are) deaf, dumb and blind.

[*Sūrah al-Baqarah* (2) : 171]

وَمِنْهُم مَّن
يَسْتَمِعُونَ إِلَيْكَ ۚ أَفَأَنتَ تُسْمِعُ ٱلصُّمَّ وَلَوْ كَانُوا۟ لَا يَعْقِلُونَ ﴿٤٢﴾
وَمِنْهُم مَّن يَنظُرُ إِلَيْكَ ۚ أَفَأَنتَ تَهْدِى ٱلْعُمْىَ وَلَوْ كَانُوا۟
لَا يُبْصِرُونَ ﴿٤٣﴾

And among them are some who listen to you, but can you make the deaf hear, even though they comprehend not? And among them are some who look at you, but can you guide the blind, even though they see not?

[*Sūrah Yūnus* (10) : 42-43]

وَمِنْهُم مَّن يَسْتَمِعُ إِلَيْكَ وَجَعَلْنَا عَلَىٰ
قُلُوبِهِمْ أَكِنَّةً أَن يَفْقَهُوهُ وَفِىٓ ءَاذَانِهِمْ وَقْرًا وَإِن يَرَوْاْ كُلَّ ءَايَةٍ
لَّا يُؤْمِنُواْ بِهَا حَتَّىٰٓ إِذَا جَآءُوكَ يُجَٰدِلُونَكَ يَقُولُ ٱلَّذِينَ كَفَرُوٓاْ إِنْ هَٰذَآ
إِلَّآ أَسَٰطِيرُ ٱلْأَوَّلِينَ ﴿٢٥﴾

And of them are some who listen to you; but
We have set veils on their hearts, so they understand it not, and deafness in their ears; if they
see every one of the signs they will not believe
therein, to the point that when they come to
argue with you, the disbelievers say: 'These are
nothing but tales of the men of old.'

[*Sūrah al-An'ām* (6) : 25]

So He informed us that their hearts cannot understand, and
their ears cannot hear, and they do not believe in what they
have seen of the Fire as He informed us about them when He
said,

وَقَالُواْ قُلُوبُنَا فِىٓ أَكِنَّةٍ
مِّمَّا تَدْعُونَآ إِلَيْهِ وَفِىٓ ءَاذَانِنَا وَقْرٌ وَمِنۢ بَيْنِنَا وَبَيْنِكَ حِجَابٌ

And they say: 'Our hearts are under coverings
from that which you invite us to, and in our ears
is deafness, and between us and you is a screen.'

[*Sūrah Fuṣṣilat* (41) : 5]

So they mentioned the barriers upon their hearts, ears and
eyes. Their bodies are alive - hearing and seeing, but this is a life
of the body devoid of life in the heart - like the life of an animal

- for the animals possess hearing and seeing, and eat and drink and marry.

This is why Allāh said,

وَمَثَلُ ٱلَّذِينَ كَفَرُوا۟ كَمَثَلِ ٱلَّذِى يَنْعِقُ
بِمَا لَا يَسْمَعُ إِلَّا دُعَآءً وَنِدَآءً ۚ صُمٌّۢ بُكْمٌ عُمْىٌ فَهُمْ لَا يَعْقِلُونَ

The example of those who disbelieve, is as that of him who shouts to the (flock of sheep) that hears nothing but calls and cries.

[*Sūrah al-Baqarah* (2) : 171]

Likening them to the cattle, at whom the shepherd shouts, and they hear nothing except the cry (not understanding what is said), as He said in other verses,

أَمْ تَحْسَبُ أَنَّ أَكْثَرَهُمْ يَسْمَعُونَ أَوْ يَعْقِلُونَ ۚ إِنْ هُمْ إِلَّا
كَٱلْأَنْعَٰمِ ۖ بَلْ هُمْ أَضَلُّ سَبِيلًا ﴿٤٤﴾

Or do you think that most of them hear or understand? They are only like cattle - nay, they are even farther astray from the Path.

[*Sūrah al-Furqān* (25) : 44]

وَلَقَدْ ذَرَأْنَا لِجَهَنَّمَ كَثِيرًا مِّنَ ٱلْجِنِّ وَٱلْإِنسِ ۖ لَهُمْ قُلُوبٌ
لَّا يَفْقَهُونَ بِهَا وَلَهُمْ أَعْيُنٌ لَّا يُبْصِرُونَ بِهَا وَلَهُمْ ءَاذَانٌ لَّا يَسْمَعُونَ
بِهَآ ۚ أُو۟لَٰٓئِكَ كَٱلْأَنْعَٰمِ بَلْ هُمْ أَضَلُّ ۚ أُو۟لَٰٓئِكَ هُمُ ٱلْغَٰفِلُونَ ﴿١٧٩﴾

And indeed We have created many of the jinn and Mankind for Hell. They have hearts where-

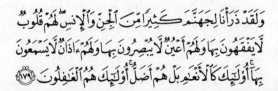

with they understand not, they have eyes wherewith they hear not. They are like cattle - nay even more astray...

[*Sūrah al-A'rāf* (7) : 179]

A group of the commentators, when referring to these verses and those that resembled them such as the verse,

وَإِذَا مَسَّ
ٱلْإِنسَـٰنَ ٱلضُّرُّ دَعَانَا لِجَنۢبِهِۦٓ أَوْ قَاعِدًا أَوْ قَآئِمًا فَلَمَّا كَشَفْنَا
عَنْهُ ضُرَّهُۥ مَرَّ كَأَن لَّمْ يَدْعُنَآ إِلَىٰ ضُرٍّ مَّسَّهُۥ

And when harm touches man, he invokes Us, lying down on his side, or sitting or standing. But when We have removed his harm from him, he passes on his way as if he has never invoked Us for a harm that touched him!

[*Sūrah Yūnus* (10) : 12]

Regarding these and other such verses that mention the faults of man and their condemnation, (the commentators) said,

> These verses refer to the disbelievers, and that the meaning of 'man' here is 'the disbelievers.'

So the one who hears this explanation is left thinking that one who openly manifests Islām is not included in this condemnation and threat, rather his thoughts link (these verses) to those who openly manifested *shirk* from amongst the Arabs, or to those he knows to have openly shown disbelief such as the Jews, the Christians and the polytheists of Turkey and India - and hence he would not benefit from these verses that Allāh revealed so that His servants may be guided.

So it is said in reply that firstly: those that openly manifest Islām include amongst them the believer and hypocrite, and the hypocrites are many in all periods of time and they are in the lowest level of the Hellfire.

Secondly: man possesses a strain of hypocrisy and disbelief even if he possesses faith along with this, as the Prophet (ﷺ) said in the *ḥadīth* reported by both al-Bukhārī and Muslim,

> There are four qualities which if found in a person make him a pure hypocrite, and the one who has a portion of them has a portion of hypocrisy until he leaves them: when he speaks he lies, when he is entrusted, he betrays, when he speaks, he speak a lie, when he makes a covenant, he proves treacherous, when he quarrels, he behaves in a evil and insulting manner [6]

So he informed us that the one who has a portion of these then he has a portion of hypocrisy, and it is established in the *Ṣaḥīḥ* of al-Bukhārī that he said to Abū Dhār,

> Indeed you have displayed a trait of *Jāhiliyyah* in you.[7]

---

[6] *Ṣaḥīḥ al-Bukhārī* [Eng. Trans. 1/32 no. 33,] and *Ṣaḥīḥ Muslim* [Eng. Trans. 1/40 no. 111].

[7] Referring to the *ḥadīth* reported by al-Ma'rūr that, 'At ar-Rabadha I met Abū Dhār (*raḍiyAllāhu 'anhu*), who was wearing a cloak and likewise his slave. I asked about the reason for this. He replied, 'I abused a person by calling his mother with bad name.' The Prophet (ﷺ) said to me, 'O Abū Dhār! Did you abuse him

And Abū Dhār was from the most truthful of people with respect to his faith. He (ﷺ) said in the authentic *aḥādīth*,

> Four (traits) in my *Ummah* are from the matters of *jāhiliyyah* (pre-Islamic ignorance): boasting about noble descent, abusing the lineage, wailing [over the dead] and seeking rain from the stars. [8]

> You will indeed follow the ways of those that came before you, inch by inch such that if they were to enter a lizard hole, you too would do so. They asked, 'Do you mean the Jews and Christians?' He replied, 'Who else?'[9]

> What the early nations took to shall also be taken to by my nation, cubit by cubit and handspan by handspan. They said, 'Do you mean the Persians and the Romans.' To which he replied, 'Who else from amongst the people could it be.'[10]

Ibn Abī Mulaykah said,

---

by calling his mother with bad names? You have displayed a trait of *Jāhiliyyah*. Your slaves are your brothers and Allāh has placed them under your command. So whoever has a brother under his command should feed him of what he eats and dress him of what he wears. Do not ask slaves to do things beyond their capacity and if you do so, then help them.' *Ṣaḥīḥ al-Bukhārī* [Eng. Trans. 1/29 no. 29] [Translator's Note]

[8] *Ṣaḥīḥ Muslim* [Eng. Trans. 2/444 no. 2033].

[9] *Ṣaḥīḥ al-Bukhārī* [Eng. Trans. 9/314 no. 422], *Ṣaḥīḥ Muslim* [Eng. Trans. 4/1402 no. 6448], Aḥmad [2/450].

[10] Refer to *Iqtiḍā Ṣirāṭ al-Mustaqīm* of Ibn Taymiyyah.

> I met thirty of the Companions of Muḥammad (ﷺ) all of them fearing hypocrisy for themselves. [11]

And from ʿAlī - or Hudhayfah - that he said,

> The heart are of four types: the clear heart that is illuminated by a torch - this is the heart of the believer. The encased heart - this is the heart of the disbeliever, the inverted heart - this is the heart of the hypocrite, and the heart that has two attractions, a time when it is called to faith, and a time when it is called to hypocrisy - these are a people that have mixed good actions with evil ones.

So when this is understood, it becomes known that every servant benefits from what Allāh mentioned concerning faith, either extolling the branches of faith or censuring the branches of disbelief.

The case mentioned above is similar to what some of them ask concerning His saying,

ٱهْدِنَا ٱلصِّرَٰطَ ٱلْمُسْتَقِيمَ ﴿٦﴾

Guide us to the Straight Path.

[*Sūrah al-Fātiḥah* (1): 6]

saying: 'Allāh has already guided the believer, so what benefit is there in seeking guidance?' Then some of them reply by saying that the meaning is 'keep us firm upon guidance' as the Arab would say to the one who is asleep, 'sleep until I come to you.'

[11] Reported by al-Bukhārī and Muslim.

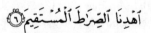

Others from amongst them say that the meaning is, 'keep our hearts firm upon the guidance' and that the request for firmness has been omitted. Yet others from amongst them say that it means, 'increase me in guidance.'

This question really occurs due to the absence of their contemplating upon the Straight Path to which the servant seeks guidance to, for the meaning [of the verse] is [seeking guidance to] act according to what Allāh ordered, and leave what He forbade in all matters.

[1.9 The Need for Beneficial Knowledge]

This is because the person, even if he has believed that Muḥammad is the Messenger of Allāh and that the Qur'ān is the truth in a general way, is commonly in need of knowledge of that which would benefit him and harm him. He is in need of knowledge concerning what he has been commanded to do and forbidden from doing in the finer aspects of the matters and in those areas of which he has no knowledge. [Not only this but we find that] that which he does have knowledge of, he does not put the greater part of it to practice! Assuming that all of the commands and prohibitions contained in the Qur'ān and Sunnah have reached him, then the Qur'ān and Sunnah contain laws that are general and universal for which it is not possible to specify to every individual person - therefore the person has been commanded due to the likes of this to ask for guidance to the Straight Path.

Guidance to the Straight Path includes all of the following matters: cognizance of what the Messenger (ﷺ) came with in detail, cognizance of what comes under his general orders and concern for acting according to ones knowledge, for indeed just having knowledge is not a cause for attaining guidance if one does not act according to his knowledge. This is why He said to His Prophet after the treaty of *Ḥudaybiyyah*,

إِنَّا فَتَحْنَا لَكَ فَتْحًا مُّبِينًا ﴿١﴾ لِّيَغْفِرَ لَكَ اللَّهُ مَا تَقَدَّمَ مِن ذَنبِكَ
وَمَا تَأَخَّرَ وَيُتِمَّ نِعْمَتَهُ عَلَيْكَ وَيَهْدِيَكَ صِرَاطًا مُّسْتَقِيمًا ﴿٢﴾

Indeed We have given you a manifest victory. That Allāh may forgive you your sins of the past and future, complete His Favour upon you, and guide you on a Straight Path.

[*Sūrah Fatḥ* (48): 1-2]

And He said with respect to Mūsā and Harūn,

وَءَاتَيْنَٰهُمَا ٱلْكِتَٰبَ
ٱلْمُسْتَبِينَ ﴿١١٧﴾ وَهَدَيْنَٰهُمَا ٱلصِّرَٰطَ ٱلْمُسْتَقِيمَ ﴿١١٨﴾

and We gave them the clear Scripture, and guided them to the Right Path.

[*Sūrah as-Ṣāffāt* (37): 117-118]

The Muslims have differed as to what Allāh Willed from the textual matters - matters of knowledge, belief and action while all of them are agreed that Muḥammad is the truth and the Qur'ān is the truth. If all of them were to have attained guidance to the Straight Path in totality then they would never have differed. Furthermore the majority of those who know what Allāh has ordered disobey Him and do not follow His Way. If they were guided to the Straight Path in these matters then they certainly would have performed what they had been commanded to do, and left what they had been forbidden from. As for those whom Allāh guided from amongst this nation until they became from the God-Fearing Friends of Allāh, then the greatest reason for this was their supplicating to Allāh with this supplication,

ٱهْدِنَا ٱلصِّرَٰطَ ٱلْمُسْتَقِيمَ ۝٦

Guide us to the Straight Path.

[*Sūrah al-Fātiḥah* (1): 6]

in every prayer along with the knowledge of their continuous need of Allāh that He guide them on the Straight Path. So due to their continually saying this supplication and their acknowledging their continuous need of Him they became God-Fearing Friends of Allāh.

Sahl bin ʿAbdullāh at-Tustorī said,

> There is not route between a servant and Allāh closer to Him then need.

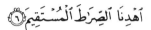

The one who has attained guidance in the past is in need of guidance in the future, this is the real meaning behind the saying of those who say that it means: 'establish us and guide us to being firm upon the Straight Path.' The opinion of those who say that it means: 'increase us in guidance' includes what has preceded. But all that has been stated refers to His guidance to the Straight Path that is to be granted in the future, for indeed action in the future is upon knowledge that is not yet attained. And the person is not considered to be one who is guided until he acts according to his knowledge in the future, but it is possible that this knowledge not be there in the future, rather it could be removed from the heart, and if it still be there it is also possible that it not be acted upon. Therefore all of mankind is in dire need of this supplication, this is why Allāh made it obligatory upon them in every prayer and they are not in need of any other supplication as they are of this one. When guidance is obtained to the Straight Path then help, provision and all of the happiness that the soul seeks are obtained [from Allāh]. Allāh knows best.

[1.10 The Reality of the Life of the Heart]

Know that the life of the heart and other than it is not merely one of sensation, movement and intent, or merely one of knowledge and ability as assumed and intent, or merely one of knowledge and ability as assumed by a group of investigators into the Knowledge of Allāh and His power such as Abū al-Ḥusain al-Baṣrī. They said:

> He can only be considered to have Life as long as He Knows and is Able.

This is not the case, rather life is an attribute existing independently in the described, and it is a condition for the existence of knowledge, intent and the ability to perform actions out of choice. Life is also a necessary outcome of these - so every living thing has understanding, intention, and everything that has knowledge, intent and performs actions and performs actions out of choice is alive.

The noun 'modesty' is derived from 'life', so the heart that is alive - it's owner is also alive - and it contains modesty which prevents it from performing evil and despicable actions, because in the modesty of the heart lies its immunity from these types of actions. This is why the Prophet (ﷺ) said,

> Modesty is from faith.[12]

and he said,

> Modesty and bashfulness are two branches from amongst the branches of faith, and obscenity and boasting are two branches from the branches of hypocrisy. [13]

This is why the living being is clearly affected by despicable actions and he has an intent that prevents him from performing them in contravention to the one who is shameless because he is not alive and therefore has no modesty and therefore no faith that would restrain him from evil. So if the heart is alive and the person dies in its separation from the body, then the death of the soul lies in its separation from the body not in the fact that it, in and of itself, has died - with the meaning of life leaving it. This is why Allāh the Exalted said,

وَلَا تَقُولُوا لِمَن يُقْتَلُ فِي سَبِيلِ ٱللَّهِ أَمْوَٰتٌۢ بَلْ أَحْيَآءٌ

> **Do not say those who are slain in the Way of Allāh: 'they are dead', rather they are alive...**
> [*Sūrah al-Baqarah* (2) : 154]

[12] *Ṣaḥīḥ al-Bukhārī* [Eng. Trans. 8/89 no. 139], *Ṣaḥīḥ Muslims* [Eng. Trans. 1/27 no. 57].

[13] Reported by at-Tirmidhī and al-Baghawī in *Sharḥ as-Sunnah* [12/366], declared *ṣaḥīḥ* by al-Ḥākim and *ḥasan* by al-ʿIrāqī.

وَلَا تَحْسَبَنَّ ٱلَّذِينَ قُتِلُوا۟ فِى
سَبِيلِ ٱللَّهِ أَمْوَٰتًۢا ۚ بَلْ أَحْيَآءٌ عِندَ رَبِّهِمْ يُرْزَقُونَ ﴿١٦٩﴾

Think not of those who are slain in the Way of Allāh as dead. Nay they are alive...

[*Sūrah Āl ʿImrān* (3) : 169]

Despite the fact that they have died are included in His sayings,

كُلُّ نَفْسٍ ذَآئِقَةُ ٱلْمَوْتِ

Every soul shall taste of death...

[*Sūrah Āl ʿImrān* (3) : 185]

إِنَّكَ مَيِّتٌ وَإِنَّهُم مَّيِّتُونَ

Indeed you will die and they will die...

[*Sūrah az-Zumar* (39) : 30]

وَهُوَ ٱلَّذِىٓ أَحْيَاكُمْ
ثُمَّ يُمِيتُكُمْ ثُمَّ يُحْيِيكُمْ ۗ إِنَّ ٱلْإِنسَٰنَ لَكَفُورٌ ﴿٦٦﴾

He is the One Who gave you life, then will cause you to die, then give you life.

[*Sūrah al-Ḥajj* (22) : 66]

Therefore the death that is affirmed is not the same as the negated death.

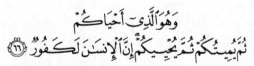

The affirmed death is the separation of the soul from the body, and the negated death is the leaving of life in totality from the

body and soul. This is similar to the fact that sleep is the brother of death. Allāh said,

ٱللَّهُ يَتَوَفَّى ٱلْأَنفُسَ حِينَ مَوْتِهَا وَٱلَّتِى لَمْ تَمُتْ فِى مَنَامِهَا فَيُمْسِكُ ٱلَّتِى قَضَىٰ عَلَيْهَا ٱلْمَوْتَ وَيُرْسِلُ ٱلْأُخْرَىٰٓ إِلَىٰٓ أَجَلٍ مُّسَمًّى

It is Allāh Who takes away the souls at the time of their death, and those that die not during their sleep. He keeps those (souls) for which He ordained death and sends the rest for a term appointed.

[*Sūrah az-Zumar* (39) :42]

The Prophet (ﷺ) used to say when he awoke from sleep,

«الْحَمْدُ للهِ الَّذِي أَحْيَانَا بَعْدَ مَا أَمَاتَنَا وَإِلَيْهِ النُّشُورُ».

All praise is due to Allāh Who gives us life after He had caused us to die and unto Him is the resurrection. [14]

In another *ḥadīth*,

«الْحَمْدُ للهِ الَّذِي عَافَانِي فِي جَسَدِي، وَرَدَّ عَلَيَّ رُوحِي، وَأَذِنَ لِي بِذِكْرِهِ».

All praise is due to Allāh Who restored to me health and returned my soul and has allowed me to re-

[14] *Ṣaḥīḥ al-Bukhārī* [Eng. Trans. 8/217], *Ṣaḥīḥ Muslim* [Eng. Trans. 4/1422 no. 6549], *Sunan Abū Dāwūd* [Eng. Trans. 3/1402 no. 5031].

member Him.[15]

When he lay down to sleep he said,

«اللَّهُمَّ إِنَّكَ خَلَقْتَ نَفْسِي وَأَنْتَ تَوَفَّاهَا، لَكَ مَمَاتُهَا وَمَحْيَاهَا، إِنْ أَحْيَيْتَهَا فَاحْفَظْهَا، وَإِنْ أَمَتَّهَا فَاغْفِرْ لَهَا. اللَّهُمَّ إِنِّي أَسْأَلُكَ الْعَافِيَةَ».

O Allāh, verily You have created my soul, and You shall take its life, to You belongs its death and life. If You should keep my soul alive then protect it, and if You should take its life then forgive it. O Allāh I ask You to grant me good health. [16]

He said,

«بِاسْمِكَ اللَّهُمَّ أَمُوتُ وأَحْيَا»

With Your Name, O Allāh, I die and live. [17]

---

[15] Reported by at-Tirmidhī [no.3401]. It is *ṣaḥīḥ* , refer to *Muḥadhdhab 'Amāl al-Yawm wa Laylā* of Shaykh 'Alī Ḥasan [pg. 33] [Translator's Note].

[16] *Ṣaḥīḥ Muslim* [Eng. Trans. 4/1422 no. 6550] from the *ḥadīth* of Ibn 'Umar.

[17] *Ṣaḥīḥ al-Bukhārī* [Eng. Trans.8/217 no.324], *Ṣaḥīḥ Muslim* [Eng. Trans. 4/1422 no, 6549].

CHAPTER II

Envy is a Sickness of the Heart

Some people said while explaining its meaning:

> 'Envy (*ḥasad*) is a grievance that befalls one due to knowledge of the good condition of the wealthy.'

So in accordance with this it is not possible that the person upon whom the blessings have been bestowed be jealous of these blessings because this person has them and is accustomed to them.

A group of people said:

> 'It is a desire to have the blessings removed from the one who is envied even if the one who is jealous does not attain the likes of these blessings.'

This is different from *ghubṭa*[1] (also meaning envy) because it refers to a desire to possess the blessings bestowed upon the one who is envied but without the desire to see them removed from him.

---

[1] *Ghubṭa*: envy, referring to the permissible form of envy where the envier wishes to have the same blessings as the envied but without desiring to see them removed from the envied. This is opposed to *ḥasad*, the blameworthy form of envy where the envier wishes to see the blessings removed from the envied.

[2.1 The Types of *Ḥasad*]

Strictly speaking, envy (*ḥasad*) is hatred and disliking the good condition of the envied one. This of two types:

1) Unrestricted dislike of the blessings bestowed upon the envied. This is the type of jealousy which incurs blame, so when one hates something he is then hurt and grieved by the existence of what he hates, and this becomes a sickness in his heart such that he takes pleasure in removal of the blessings from the envied even if this does not result in any benefit to him except for the single benefit of having the pain that was in his soul removed. But this pain is not removed except as a result of his continuously watching the envied so that the jealous person finds relief when the blessing is removed, but then it becomes more severe as is the case of the one who is sick, for it is possible that this blessing, or one similar to it, returns to the envied. This is why this second group said:

> 'It is a desire to have the blessings removed,'

for indeed the one who dislikes the blessings bestowed upon other than him desires to see them removed.

2) That he dislikes the superiority of that person over him, and he desires to be like him or better, so this is jealousy and has been called *ghubṭa*, and the Prophet (ﷺ) called it *ḥasad* in the *ḥadīth* reported by both al-Bukhārī and Muslim from the *ḥadīth* of Ibn Masʿūd and Ibn ʿUmar, (*raḍiyAllāhu ʿanhum*), that he (ﷺ) said:

> There is no envy (*ḥasad*) except in two cases: a per-

> son to whom Allāh has granted wisdom, and he rules by this and teaches it to the people, and a person to whom Allāh has granted wealth and property and along with this the power to spend it in the cause of Truth. [2]

This being the wording of Ibn Mas'ūd. The wording of Ibn 'Umar, (*raḍiyAllāhu 'anhumā*) is,

> A person to whom Allāh has given the Qur'ān and he recites it night and day, and a person to whom Allāh has granted wealth and property from which he gives in charity night and day. [3]

Al-Bukhārī also reports this *ḥadīth* from Abū Hurayrah (*raḍiyAllāhu 'anhu*) and its wording is,

> There is no desirable form of jealousy except for two types: a person to whom Allāh has given the Qur'ān and he recites it day and night, so when a person hears him he says, 'If only I were given the likes of what he has been given so that I may act upon it the way this person is.' And a person to whom Allāh has bestowed wealth and he spends in the cause of Truth, so a person says, 'If only I were given the likes of what he has been given, so that I may act upon it the way this person is.' [4]

---

[2] *Ṣaḥīḥ al-Bukhārī* [Eng. Trans. 1/62 no. 73], *Ṣaḥīḥ Muslim* [Eng. Trans. 2/389 no. 1779].

[3] *Ṣaḥīḥ al-Bukhārī* [Eng. Trans. 6/500 no. 543], *Ṣaḥīḥ Muslim* [Eng. Trans. 2/388 no. 1777].

[4] *Ṣaḥīḥ al-Bukhārī* [Eng. Trans. 6/501 no. 544].

So the Prophet (ﷺ) forbade *ḥasad*, with the exception of two cases which are referred to as al-*ghubṭa*, meaning that a person love the condition of someone else and dislike that this person be superior in this way (without his wishing that it be removed from that person).

So if it is asked: 'Then why is this called envy when he loves only that Allāh bestows these blessings upon him?' It is said, 'The starting point of this love is his looking towards the favours Allāh has bestowed upon someone else and his disliking that this person be favoured over him. So if this other person were not present then he would not have desired these blessings. So because the starting point of this love is this dislike that someone else be made superior to him, then this is called envy due to the love following the dislike. As for desiring that Allāh bestows favours upon him without consideration of people's material conditions then this is not envy at all.'

This is why the generality of mankind have been tried with this second type of envy that has also been called *al-munāfasah* (competition) because two people compete in a single desired matter, both of them trying to attain the same good. The reason for their trying to attain it is that one of them dislikes that the other be blessed with this matter over him just as any one of two competitors dislikes that other beat him.

Competition is not considered blameworthy in general, rather it is considered to be praiseworthy when competing for righteousness, the Exalted said,

﴿٢١﴾ إِنَّ ٱلۡأَبۡرَارَ لَفِي نَعِيمٍ ﴿٢٢﴾ عَلَى ٱلۡأَرَآئِكِ يَنظُرُونَ ﴿٢٣﴾ تَعۡرِفُ فِي
وُجُوهِهِمۡ نَضۡرَةَ ٱلنَّعِيمِ ﴿٢٤﴾ يُسۡقَوۡنَ مِن رَّحِيقٖ مَّخۡتُومٍ ﴿٢٥﴾
يُسۡقَوۡنَ مِن رَّحِيقٖ مَّخۡتُومٍ ﴿٢٥﴾

Indeed the pious will be in delight. On thrones, looking on. You will recognize in their faces the brightness of delight. They will be given to drink pure sealed wine. The last thereof (that wine) will be the smell of Musk, and for this let those compete who want to compete.

[*Sūrah al-Muṭaffifīn* (83):22-26]

So one is commanded to compete for these delights and not to compete for the delight of this fleeting world. This is in total agreement to the *ḥadīth* of the Prophet (ﷺ), for he forbade envy except of the one who has been granted knowledge and he acts according to it and teaches it, and the one who has been bestowed wealth and spends it (in the way of Allāh). As for the one who has been granted knowledge but does not act upon this knowledge, or the one who has been bestowed wealth but does not spend this is obedience to Allāh, then such a person is not to be envied and neither is his condition to be hoped for, for he is not in a state of good that is desirable, rather he is being presented with punishment. He also allowed jealousy for the one who has been given a responsibility and he fulfils it with knowledge and justice, and fulfils the trusts of its owners, and judges amongst the people by the Qur'ān and *Sunnah*.

The station of such a person is lofty but this only comes after a great amount of effort (*jihād*) - the same is true of the *mujāhid*.

But the souls do not envy the one who is in severe hardship and this is why the Prophet (ﷺ) did not mention it even though the *mujāhid*, fighting in the Way of Allāh, is superior to the one who is spending wealth. The opposite is true for the teacher and spender for they have no enemy in the physical world, but in the case that there were an enemy that they would have to perform *jihād* against, then their ranking is more superior (than their station without having an enemy to fight). Similarly the Prophet (ﷺ) did not mention the one who prays, fasts and performs the pilgrimage, because there is no tangible benefit attained from the people for these actions by which the person can be exalted or disgraced, as can be attained in teaching and spending.

[2.2 Between *Ḥasad* and *Ghubṭa*]

Fundamentally, envy occurs when someone else attains power and authority; otherwise the one who is performing actions is not normally envied, even if this person be blessed with far more food, drink and wives than others, as opposed to these two blessings of power and authority, for they cause a great deal of envy. This is why you find envy directed at the People of Knowledge, who have a following amongst the people that you will not find directed to others who do not have such a following. Similarly for the one who attracts a following due to his spending his wealth, for the people benefit this person by nourishing his heart, and this person brings benefit to them by nourishment of the bodies. Mankind is in need of that which will correct them in both these matters, this is why Allāh, the one free from imperfection, has propounded two parables,

ضَرَبَ ٱللَّهُ مَثَلًا عَبۡدًا
مَّمۡلُوكًا لَّا يَقۡدِرُ عَلَىٰ شَيۡءٖ وَمَن رَّزَقۡنَٰهُ مِنَّا رِزۡقًا حَسَنًا
فَهُوَ يُنفِقُ مِنۡهُ سِرًّا وَجَهۡرًاۖ هَلۡ يَسۡتَوُۥنَۚ ٱلۡحَمۡدُ لِلَّهِۚ
بَلۡ أَكۡثَرُهُمۡ لَا يَعۡلَمُونَ ﴿٧٥﴾ وَضَرَبَ ٱللَّهُ مَثَلٗا رَّجُلَيۡنِ
أَحَدُهُمَآ أَبۡكَمُ لَا يَقۡدِرُ عَلَىٰ شَيۡءٖ وَهُوَ كَلٌّ عَلَىٰ
مَوۡلَىٰهُ أَيۡنَمَا يُوَجِّههُّ لَا يَأۡتِ بِخَيۡرٍۖ هَلۡ يَسۡتَوِي هُوَ وَمَن
يَأۡمُرُ بِٱلۡعَدۡلِ وَهُوَ عَلَىٰ صِرَٰطٖ مُّسۡتَقِيمٖ ﴿٧٦﴾

Allāh puts forward the example: a slave under the possession of another, he has no power of any sort, and (the other) a man on whom We have bestowed a good provision from Us, and he spends thereof secretly and openly. Could they be equal? (By no means, not). All the praises and thanks be to Allāh. Nay! (But) most of them know not. And Allāh puts forward another parable of two men, one of them dumb, who has no power over anything, and he is a burden to his master, whichever way he directs him he brings no good. Is such a man equal to one who commands justice, and is himself on the Straight Path?

[*Sūrah al-Naḥl* (16):75-76]

These two parables were propounded by Allāh for His Own Holy Self and for that which is worshipped besides Him, for indeed the idols are not capable of performing any actions that would be of benefit, and neither of saying anything that would be of benefit. So when a completely powerless slave under the possession of someone is considered, and another to whom Allāh has provided a goodly provision from which he spends in secret and in the open, can this slave, incapable of doing good, and this person capable of doing good for the people in secret and open, ever be equal? And He, free is as He from defect, is able to bestow good upon His servants, and as He is continuously doing so. So how can this incapable slave (i.e. the idol) who cannot do anything, be likened to Allāh to the extent that he is worshipped alongside Him? So this is the parable of one to whom Allāh has bestowed wealth from which he spends day and night.

The second parable: when two people are considered, one of them is dumb, he does not understand nor speak, and is not capable of anything and is in fact a burden upon his master, for whichever way he directs him he brings no good and hence he is of absolutely no use. The other is a just scholar - enjoining justice and acting justly, and is upon the Straight Path. This person is then like the one upon whom Allāh has conferred wisdom and he acts according to it and teaches it. And Allāh has propounded this parable for Himself, for He is All-Knowing, All-Just, All-Powerful, commanding justice, He is maintaining His creation is justice is upon the Straight Way as He, the Exalted said,

شَهِدَ اللَّهُ أَنَّهُ لَا إِلَٰهَ إِلَّا هُوَ وَالْمَلَائِكَةُ وَأُولُو الْعِلْمِ قَائِمًا بِالْقِسْطِ ۚ
لَا إِلَٰهَ إِلَّا هُوَ الْعَزِيزُ الْحَكِيمُ ﴿١٨﴾

Allāh bears witness that there is none worthy of

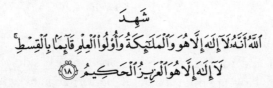

worship but He, and the angels, and those having knowledge; (He is always) maintaining His creation in Justice. There is none worthy of worship but He, the All-Mighty, the All-Wise.

[*Sūrah Āl 'Imrān* (3):18.]

And He said upon the tongue of Hūd,

إِنَّ رَبِّي عَلَىٰ صِرَٰطٍ مُّسْتَقِيمٍ

Indeed my Lord is upon the Straight Path.

[*Sūrah Hūd* (11):56]

This is why the people used to exalt the home of al-'Abbās: 'Abdullāh used to teach the people and his brother used to feed them, and so they used to exalt them due to this.

Mu'āwiyah, (*raḍiyAllāhu 'anhu*), saw the people asking Ibn 'Umar about the rites of Ḥajj and Ibn 'Umar would give them the verdicts, to which Mu'āwiyah said, 'By Allāh this is nobility' or something similar.

[2.3 The Competition between *aṯ-Ṣiddīq* and 'Umar]

So here is 'Umar bin al-Khaṭṭāb (*raḍiyAllāhu 'anhu*) competing with Abū Bakr (*raḍiyAllāhu 'anhu*) with respect to spending in charity as is established in the *Ṣaḥīḥ* (of al-Bukhārī) from 'Umar bin al-Khaṭṭāb, (*raḍiyAllāhu 'anhu*), that he said:

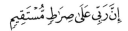

> The Messenger of Allāh (ﷺ) commanded us to give in charity, and this coincided with my possessing some wealth. So I said (to myself): 'If there is a day that I can better Abū Bakr than it is this one.' So I

> went with half of my wealth and the Messenger of Allāh (ﷺ) asked me, 'What have you left for your family?' I replied, 'The same amount.' Then Abū Bakr came with everything that he possessed and the Messenger of Allāh (ﷺ) asked him, 'What have you left for your family?' He replied, 'I have left Allāh and His Messenger for them.' So I said, 'I will never be able to better you in anything!'

So what 'Umar did here was competition and the permitted type of jealousy (*ghubṭa*), but the state of *aṣ-Ṣiddīq* was better than his, and thus he would generally be the victor in such competition due to his indifference to the condition of others.

[2.4 Moses Displays *Ghubṭa*]

Likewise is the case with Prophet Mūsā as is mentioned in the *ḥadīth* of *Mi'rāj* that he competed and felt jealousy towards the Prophet (ﷺ) to the point that he,

> Cried due to the extent to which the Prophet (ﷺ) has surpassed him. So it was said to him, 'Why are you crying?' He replied, 'I am crying because there is a servant who shall be sent after me, and more of his nation shall enter Paradise than mine.' [5]

This *ḥadīth* is also reported in other than the *Ṣaḥīḥ* with a different wording,

> We passed a person while he was saying in a loud voice, 'You have blessed him and honoured him

[5] Reported by both al-Bukhārī and Muslim

> (over me).' So we were raised to him and gave him our salām, he replied to our salām and said, 'Who is this with you O Jibrā'īl?' He said, 'This is Aḥmad.' He said, 'Welcome O Illiterate Prophet who has conveyed the Message of his Lord and sincerely advised his nation.' Then we moved on and I said, 'Who was this O Jibrā'īl?' He replied, 'That was Mūsā bin 'Imrān.' I said, 'And who was he censuring?' He replied, 'He was censuring your Lord with regards to you.' I said, 'He was raising his voice to His Lord?' He replied, 'Indeed Allāh knew his truthfulness.'

So in this 'Umar resembled Mūsā, and the condition of our Prophet (ﷺ) was superior to that of Mūsā for he did not possess any of this permissible jealousy.

[2.5 Whoevers Ranking Becomes Lofty, He is Secured from *Ghubṭa*]

Similar to this from amongst the *Ṣaḥābah* were Abū 'Ubaydah bin Jarrāḥ and those like him who were free from these types of concerns and due to this they were of a more exalted rank than those who would compete and display jealousy (*ghubṭa*) even though it was permitted. This is why Abū 'Ubaydah deserved to be called,

> The trusted one of this *Ummah*.[6]

For if the one trusted does not have any rivalry and desire in his self for the things that he is entrusted with, then he is the

[6] Reported by both al-Bukhārī and Muslim

most deserving of having the trust placed in him. The one who is known to possess no rivalry in greater matters is entrusted with the smaller matters, and the one is known to have no reason to steal from the wealth is entrusted with the wealth. As for the one who finds in himself treachery that resembles that of a wolf entrusted with sheep, then he is not able to discharge the trust placed in him due to his having in his heart a desire for what he is entrusted with.

It is reported in the *Musnad* of Aḥmad from Anas, (*raḍiyAllāhu 'anhu*), that he said,

> We were sitting in the presence of the Messenger of Allāh (ﷺ) one day and he said, 'A person is about to arrive from this mountain path who is from the people of Paradise.' So a person from the Anṣār arrived, his beard dripping with the water of wuḍū and holding his sandals in his left hand, and he gave us the salām. The next day the Prophet (ﷺ) said words of similar import and the same person appeared in the same condition. On the third day the Prophet (ﷺ) again said words of similar import and again this person appeared in the same condition, so when the Prophet (ﷺ) left, 'Abdullāh bin 'Amr al-'Āṣ followed this person and said, 'indeed I have abused my father and I swore that I would not go to him for three days so if you would let me stay with you until those three days expire, I would do so.' He replied, 'Yes.'

Anas continued saying,

> So ʿAbdullāh told us that he spend three nights with this person yet he did not see him stand for the night prayer at all. All he did was when he turned sides on his bed he would mention Allāh and make *takbīr* and would do this until he stood for the *Fajr* prayer. ʿAbdullāh said, 'Except that I never heard him speak except good.' So when the three days were over I was eager to make little of his actions. I said, 'O servant of Allāh there was no hatred or disassociation between my father and me but I heard the Messenger of Allāh (ﷺ) saying on three occasions, 'A person is about to arrive who is from the people of Paradise,' and you arrived on those three occasions, so I wished to stay with you so that I may look at your actions and emulate them. But I have not seen you perform a great deal of actions, so what is it that has reached you to make the Messenger of Allāh (ﷺ) say what he said?' He replied, 'It is nothing more than what you have seen, except that I do not find in myself any disloyalty to any of the Muslims, and neither do I find any jealousy for the wealth that Allāh has bestowed upon them.' ʿAbdullāh said, 'This is that which has reached you and is something that we cannot endure.'[7]

So in the saying of ʿAbdullāh bin ʿAmr to him, 'This is something that has reached you and something that we cannot endure' lies an indication of his lack of jealousy and his being secure from all types of jealousy. This is why Allāh praised the *Anṣār* with His saying,

[7] Its *isnād* is *ṣaḥīḥ*

وَلَا يَجِدُونَ فِى صُدُورِهِمْ حَاجَةً
مِّمَّآ أُوتُوا۟ وَيُؤْثِرُونَ عَلَىٰٓ أَنفُسِهِمْ وَلَوْ كَانَ بِهِمْ خَصَاصَةٌ

And have no jealousy in their breasts for that which they have been given (the *muhājirṭ n*), and give them preference over themselves even though they were in need of that.

[*Sūrah al-Ḥashr* (59):9]

Meaning that which has been given to their brothers from the *Muhājirūn*. The scholars of *tafsīr* have stated:

> 'They do not find in their breasts jealousy and hatred for what has been given to the *Muhājirūn*.'

Then some of them said,

> 'What has been given to them from the war booty.'

And others said:

> 'What has been given to them of precedence and blessings'

So they find no need of that which has been given the *Muhājirūn* of wealth and rank even though jealousy arises over these sorts of things.

Between the Aws and the Khazraj there existed competition in matters of religion, such that if one tribe were to do something for which they were regarded favourably by Allāh and His

Messenger then the other tribe would desire to do the same. So this is competition in that which would bring them closer to Allāh.

Allāh says,

خِتَٰمُهُۥ مِسۡكٞۚ وَفِي ذَٰلِكَ فَلۡيَتَنَافَسِ ٱلۡمُتَنَٰفِسُونَ ٢٦

...Then for this let those who compete, compete!

[*Sūrah al-Muṭaffifīn* (83):26]

[2.6 Blameworthy Jealousy]

As for the jealousy that is totally blameworthy then Allāh has said with regards to the Jews,

وَدَّ كَثِيرٞ مِّنۡ أَهۡلِ
ٱلۡكِتَٰبِ لَوۡ يَرُدُّونَكُم مِّنۢ بَعۡدِ إِيمَٰنِكُمۡ كُفَّارًا حَسَدٗا
مِّنۡ عِندِ أَنفُسِهِم مِّنۢ بَعۡدِ مَا تَبَيَّنَ لَهُمُ ٱلۡحَقُّۖ

Many of the People of the Book wish that if they could turn you away as disbelievers after you have believed, out of envy from their own selves even after the truth has become clear to them.

[*Sūrah al-Baqarah* (2):109]

'They wish' meaning that they hope to make you apostasise from your religion out of jealousy. So jealousy was the deciding factor behind their wish even after the Truth has been made clear to them. This is because when they saw you attain what you attained of blessings - in fact they saw you attain that which they themselves had never attained - they became jealous of you. Similarly this is mentioned in another verse,

أَمْ
يَحْسُدُونَ ٱلنَّاسَ عَلَىٰ مَآ ءَاتَىٰهُمُ ٱللَّهُ مِن فَضْلِهِۦ ۖ فَقَدْ ءَاتَيْنَآ
ءَالَ إِبْرَٰهِيمَ ٱلْكِتَـٰبَ وَٱلْحِكْمَةَ وَءَاتَيْنَـٰهُم مُّلْكًا عَظِيمًا ﴿٥٤﴾
فَمِنْهُم مَّنْ ءَامَنَ بِهِۦ وَمِنْهُم مَّن صَدَّ عَنْهُ ۚ وَكَفَىٰ بِجَهَنَّمَ سَعِيرًا

Or do they envy men for what Allāh has given them of His bounty? Then We have already given the family of Abraham the Book and Wisdom, and conferred upon them a great kingdom. Of them were (some) who believed in him (Muḥammad) and of them were some who averted their faces from him, and enough is Hell for burning (them)...

[*Sūrah an-Nisā'* (4):54-55]

قُلْ أَعُوذُ بِرَبِّ ٱلْفَلَقِ ﴿١﴾ مِن شَرِّ مَا خَلَقَ ﴿٢﴾ وَمِن
شَرِّ غَاسِقٍ إِذَا وَقَبَ ﴿٣﴾ وَمِن شَرِّ ٱلنَّفَّـٰثَـٰتِ فِى
ٱلْعُقَدِ ﴿٤﴾ وَمِن شَرِّ حَاسِدٍ إِذَا حَسَدَ ﴿٥﴾

Say: I seek refuge with the Lord of the Daybreak. From the evil of what He has created. And from the evil of the darkening (night) as it comes with its darkness. And from the evil of the witchcrafts when they blow in the knots. And from the evil of the envier when he envies.

[*Sūrah al-Falaq* (113):1-5]

A group of scholars of *tafsīr* mentioned that this *Sūrah* was revealed due to the jealousy of the jews harboured towards the Messenger of Allāh (ﷺ) to the extent that they performed magic on him. The magic was done by the Jew, Labīd bin al-'Aṣam.[8]

So the one who is jealous, hating the favours bestowed by Allāh upon someone else is an oppressor, going beyond bounds due to this. As for the one who dislikes that someone else be blessed and wishes to be blessed in the same way, then this is forbidden for him except in that which will bring him closer to Allāh. So if he were to wish for something that has been given to someone else which would help bring him closer to Allāh then there is no problem in this. However, his wishing for it in his heart, without looking to the condition of someone else is better and more excellent.

Then if this person were to act, dictated by this jealousy, he would be an oppressor going beyond bounds, deserving of punishment unless he repents. So the one who is affected by the one who is jealous is oppressed and should be enjoined to patience and *taqwā*. He should be patient of the harm afflicted upon him by the one who is jealous, and he should forgive and overlook, just as Allāh said,

[8] As is reported by al-Bukhārī, Muslim and Aḥmad. Refer to the *tafsīr* of Ibn Kathīr (4/584).

وَدَّ كَثِيرٌ مِّنۡ أَهۡلِ
ٱلۡكِتَٰبِ لَوۡ يَرُدُّونَكُم مِّنۢ بَعۡدِ إِيمَٰنِكُمۡ كُفَّارًا حَسَدٗا
مِّنۡ عِندِ أَنفُسِهِم مِّنۢ بَعۡدِ مَا تَبَيَّنَ لَهُمُ ٱلۡحَقُّۖ

Many of the People of the Book wish that if they could turn you away as disbelievers after you have believed, out of envy from their own selves even after the truth has become clear to them. But forgive and overlook until Allāh brings about His Command.

[*Sūrah al-Baqarah* (2):109]

Indeed Yūsuf, (*ʿalayhis salām*) was tried by the jealousy of his brothers:

إِذۡ قَالُواْ لَيُوسُفُ وَأَخُوهُ أَحَبُّ إِلَىٰٓ
أَبِينَا مِنَّا وَنَحۡنُ عُصۡبَةٌ إِنَّ أَبَانَا لَفِي ضَلَٰلٖ مُّبِينٍ ﴿٨﴾

When they said: Truly, Yūsuf and his brother are loved more by our father than we...

[*Sūrah Yūsuf* (12):8]

So they were envied due to their father favouring them over the rest of the brothers, which is why Yaʿqūb said to Yūsuf,

قَالَ يَٰبُنَيَّ لَا تَقۡصُصۡ رُءۡيَاكَ عَلَىٰٓ إِخۡوَتِكَ فَيَكِيدُواْ لَكَ كَيۡدًاۖ
إِنَّ ٱلشَّيۡطَٰنَ لِلۡإِنسَٰنِ عَدُوّٞ مُّبِينٞ ﴿٥﴾

O my son! Relate not your vision to your broth-

ers, lest they arrange a plot against you. Indeed! Satan is an open enemy to man!

[*Sūrah Yūsuf* (12):5]

They went on to oppress him by discussing his murder and throwing him in the well, and his being sold as a slave by the ones who took him to the land of the disbelievers, and his subsequently being owned by these disbelieving people. Then after being oppressed, Yūsuf was tried by the one who invited him to an indecent deed and attempted to seduce him, and she sought aid from anyone who would help her in this but he was preserved from this. Instead he chose to be imprisoned rather than perform this indecent deed, preferring the punishment of this world rather than the Displeasure of Allāh (in the Hereafter).

Hence he was oppressed by the one who desired him due to her base desires and her corrupt objective. So this love with which she desired him arose as a result of her succumbing to the vain desires of her heart, and its happiness or sadness lay in his accepting or rejecting the temptation. He was also oppressed by those who hated him with a hatred that led to his being thrown in the well, then his becoming captive and owned without his choice, therefore these people removed him from the absolute freedom that he enjoyed to becoming forced into slavery to the false worshippers. This forced him to seek refuge in the prison out of his own free will, thereby making his trial greater.

His patience on this occasion arose out of his own volition coupled with his fear of Allāh, thus differing from his patience at their oppression, which was having patience at the onset of calamities, and if one were not to be patient at the likes of these then he would take to the way of mere animals.

This second type of patience, arising from one's free will, is the more excellent of the two. This is why Allāh said,

إِنَّهُۥ مَن يَتَّقِ وَيَصْبِرْ فَإِنَّ ٱللَّهَ لَا يُضِيعُ أَجْرَ
ٱلْمُحْسِنِينَ ﴿٩٠﴾

> **Indeed he who fears Allāh, and is patient, then surely Allāh makes not the reward of the doers of good to be lost.**
>
> [*Sūrah Yūsuf* (12):90]

Likewise when the believer is harmed due to his faith; and disbelief, transgression and disobedience is sought from him - and if he were not to accept this then he would be harmed and punished - then he should choose this harm and punishment over renegading from his religion - even if it results in imprisonment or banishment from his land - just as was done by the *Muhājirūn* in their choosing to leave their settlements rather than leave their religion for which they were harmed and punished.

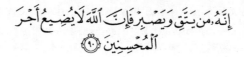

The Prophet (ﷺ) was harmed in a number of different ways but he was patient through-out this with a patience that arose out of his own volition, and indeed he was harmed in this way only that he may do what he did out of his own choice. So this patience of his was greater than the patience of Yūsuf, for only an indecent action was sought from Yūsuf, and he was only punished by imprisonment when he did not comply. But disbelief was sought from the Prophet (ﷺ) and his Companions, and when they did not do this - then they were punished by being slaughtered and other such harms - the least of which was imprisonment, for the polytheists imprisoned him and Banī Hāshim for a time in a mountain pass. Then when Abū Ṭālib died they became more severe against him, and when the *Anṣār* gave him the pledge of the allegiance and when the polytheists came to know of this they tried to prevent him from leaving (for Madīnah) and tried to detain him and his Companions. Then all of them emigrated secretly except for 'Umar bin al-Khaṭṭāb and those like him.

So what befell the believers came about as a result of their choosing obedience to Allāh and His Messenger and it was not from the afflictions that occur without the servant's choice of the type that Yūsuf was tried with, and neither of the type of his being separated from his father. So this patience endured by the believers was the nobler of the two types of patience, and its possessors are greater with respect to ranking. This, even though the one who is tried without his will shall be rewarded for his patience and his contentment with the decree of Allāh, and his sins will be expiated. As for the person who is tried and harmed for choosing obedience to Allāh, then he will be rewarded for the actual trial and it shall be written as a righteous action for him. Allāh, the Most High, said,

ذَٰلِكَ بِأَنَّهُمْ لَا يُصِيبُهُمْ ظَمَأٌ وَلَا نَصَبٌ
وَلَا مَخْمَصَةٌ فِي سَبِيلِ ٱللَّهِ وَلَا يَطَـُٔونَ مَوْطِئًا يَغِيظُ
ٱلْكُفَّارَ وَلَا يَنَالُونَ مِنْ عَدُوٍّ نَّيْلًا إِلَّا كُتِبَ لَهُم
بِهِۦ عَمَلٌ صَٰلِحٌ ۚ إِنَّ ٱللَّهَ لَا يُضِيعُ أَجْرَ ٱلْمُحْسِنِينَ ﴿١٢٠﴾

> **That is because they suffer neither thirst nor fatigue, nor hunger in the Cause of Allāh, nor do they take any step to raise the anger of disbelievers nor inflict any injury upon an enemy but it is written to their credit as a righteous deed. Indeed Allāh wastes not the reward of the doers of good.**
>
> [*Sūrah at-Tawbah* (9):120]

This contrasting with the case of the one who is tried without his choice, such as being sick, or death, or a thief stealing from him - this person shall be rewarded for his patience only, not for the actual trial itself and what results from it. As for those who are harmed due to their faith in Allāh and obedience to Him and His Messenger, and as a result of this they are in pain, or are sick, or are imprisoned, or are forced to leave their land, or their property and family is taken from them, or are beaten and abused, or their position and wealth is diminished, then in this they are upon the way of the Prophets and those that followed them such as the *Muhājirūn*.

So these people shall be rewarded for what has harmed them, and a righteous action shall be written for them due to it just as the *mujāhid* shall be rewarded for the hunger, thirst and fatigue that afflicts him, and for enraging the disbelievers even if these effects are not something he has physically set out to do, but they are resultant from his action (of performing *jihād*) that he has chosen to do. The people have differed over this: can it be said that these resultant effects are actions of the actor of the reason for these effects, or are they Actions of Allāh, or is there no actor fot them ? What is correct is that they are shared between the actor of the reason and the (Actor of the) totality of the reasons, and this is why a righteous action is written for him.

The purpose behind this discussion is that jealousy is one of the sicknesses of the soul, and it is an illness that afflicts the generality of mankind and only a few are secure from it. This is why it is said:

> The body is never free from jealousy, but debasement brings it out, and nobility hides it.

It was said to al-Ḥasan al-Baṣrī,

> 'Can a believer be envied?' He replied, 'What has made you forget Yūsuf and his brothers, have you no father?' But you should keep (this envy should it occur) blinded in your heart, for you cannot be harmed by that which you did not act upon in speech or action.'

[2.7 The Cure for Jealousy]

So the one who finds that he harbours jealousy in his soul towards someone else, then it is upon him to treat it with patience and *taqwā* of Allāh, and dislike it being in his soul. Many religious people do not take a stance against the one who is envied and neither do they help the one who would oppress him, but neither do they establish what is obligatory with respect to his rights. Rather when someone censures the one who is envied they do not agree with or aid him in the censure but neither do they mention his praiseworthy qualities. Likewise if someone were to praise him they remain silent. So these people are responsible for their leaving what is commanded with respect to the rights of the envied, and they have exceeded the proper bounds in this even though they may not have taken a stance against him. The reward of these people is that their rights in turn will be neglected and on some occasions they will not be treated fairly, and neither will they be helped against the one who oppresses them, just as they did not aid the envied who was oppressed. As for the one who actually takes a stance against the envied, either with words or actions then he will be punished for this, and the one who fears Allāh and is patient and does not become one of the oppressors - Allāh will benefit him for his *taqwā*.

[2.8 The Causes for Jealousy]

This is what occurred with Zaynab bint Jahsh (*raḍiyAllāhu ʿanhā*) for she used to be one who would vie with 'Ā'ishah from the wives of the Prophet (ﷺ). The jealousy displayed by some women to others is great, and is especially true of those who are married to one husband. The woman will go to great extents to get her allotted time from him for sometimes some of her allotted time will be missed due to his sharing with other wives. This jealousy commonly occurs amongst those that share authority or property[9] in the case when some of them take a share from it and others are left with none. It also occurs between those that debate, due to their hatred that their opponent gets the better of them, such as the jealousy of the brothers of Yūsuf, or the jealousy of the two sons of Ādam one to the other for in this case the brother was envied by the other due to Allāh accepting his sacrifice and not the other's, this leading to his mur-

[9] Or those that share knowledge, this is why the scholars of *ḥadīth* do not accept the reports of scholars criticizing their contemporaries.

der. Also, the jealousy displayed towards the Muslims by the Jews. It was said,

> The first sins by which Allāh was disobeyed were three: covetousness, arrogance and jealousy. Covetousness was displayed by Ādam, arrogance by Iblīs, and jealousy from Qābīl when he killed Hābīl. [10]

In the *ḥadīth* there occurs:

> There are three sins from which no one can be saved: jealousy, suspicion and omens. Shall I tell you of what would remove you from this: when you envy then do not hate, when you are suspicious then do not actualize your suspicions, and when you see omens then ignore them. [11]

Reported by Ibn Abī ad-Dunyā from the *ḥadīth* of Abū Hurayrah, *raḍiyAllāhu ʿanhu.*

In the *Sunan* from the Prophet (ﷺ),

> You have been afflicted with the illness of the nations that came before you - jealousy and hatred. They are the shearers, I do not mean shearers of

[10] *Ḍaʿīf*, reported by Abu ash-Shaykh and aṭ-Ṭabarānī from Ḥasan al-Baṣrī as a *mursal* report.

[11] Reported by Aḥmad [1412, 1430] and at-Tirmidhī [2512]. Its chain of narration contains unknown narrators, but the *ḥadīth* has witnesses reported by Abū ad-Dardā' and Abū Hurayrah that strengthen it. Rather to *Majmaʿ az-Zawā'id* [10/8] whose authors also refer this *ḥadīth* to al-Bazzār. Al-Mundhirī said that it *isnād* is good.

> the hair, rather they are shearers of the religion. [12]

So he called jealousy an illness just as he called miserliness an illness in his saying,

> And what illness is worse than miserliness. [13]

And in another *ḥadīth*,

> I seek refuge with You from the evil morals and manners, vain desires and illnesses.

Mentioning illnesses alongside manners and vain desires. Manners are those things that the soul becomes accustomed to such that they become its nature and disposition. Allāh said in this regard,

وَإِنَّكَ لَعَلَىٰ خُلُقٍ عَظِيمٍ ﴿٤﴾

> **And indeed you are upon an exalted standard of character.**
>
> [*Sūrah Qalam* (68):4]

Ibn 'Abbās, Ibn 'Uyaynah and Aḥmad ibn Hanbal (*raḍiyAllāhu 'anhum*) said in commentary to this:

> Meaning 'upon a great religion.'

[12] Reported by at-Tirmidhī, at-Tabarānī and al-Ḥākim who said that it was *ṣaḥīḥ* and it as he said.

[13] Reported by Aḥmad, Ḥākim and others. It is *ṣaḥīḥ*. Refer to: *Ṣaḥīḥ al-Jāmi'* [no. 7104] and the notes of Shu'ayb al-Arna'ūṭ upon *Sharḥ Muskil al-Āthār* of aṭ-Ṭaḥāwī [14/151-154]. [Translator's Note]

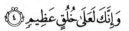

And in a variant wording of Ibn 'Abbās:

'The religion of Islām.'

This was similarly stated by 'Ā'ishah (*raḍiyAllāhu 'anhā*)

His manners were the Qur'ān,

and Ḥasan al-Baṣrī,

> The manners of the Qur'ān is 'the exalted standard of character.'

As for 'vain desires' then they are temporary anomalous conditions, and 'illness' is sickness - this is an affliction that harms the heart and corrupts it. In the first *ḥadīth* jealousy was mentioned along with hatred. This is because the envier, first of all dislikes the bounty bestowed by Allāh upon the one who is envied, and then begins hating this person. This is because the hatred of the thing being bestowed leads to hatred of the one upon whom it is bestowed, for when the blessings of Allāh are bestowed upon an individual, he would love that they go away, and they would not go away except by the one who is envied going away, therefore he hates him and loves that he not be there.

Jealousy necessarily leads to desire and hatred just as Allāh informed us of those that came before us: that they differed,

بَعْدِ مَا جَآءَهُمُ ٱلْعِلْمُ بَغْيًۢا بَيْنَهُمْ

After their came to them knowledge out of

> **mutual hatred and desire.**
>
> [*Sūrah Āl ʿImrān* (3):19]

So their differing did not arise due to the lack of knowledge, rather they knew the Truth, but it was due to some of them hating others, just as the envier hates the envied.

In *Ṣaḥīḥs* of al-Bukhārī and Muslim, Anas bin Mālik (*raḍiyAllāhu ʿanhu*) reports that the Prophet (ﷺ) said,

> Do not envy each other, do not hate each other, do not oppose each other, and do not cut relations, rather be servants of Allāh as brothers. It is not permissible for a Muslim to disassociate from his brother for more than three days such that they meet and one ignores the other, and the best of them is the one who initiates the salām. [14]

He (ﷺ) said, in the *ḥadīth* that is agreed to be authentic, reported by Anas also,

> By the One in Whose Hand is my soul, none of you believes until he loves for his brother what he loves for himself. [15]

Allāh, the Most High, said,

---

[14] *Ṣaḥīḥ al-Bukhārī* [Eng. Trans. 8/58 no. 91], *Ṣaḥīḥ Muslim* [Eng. Trans. 4/1360 no. 6205, 6210].

[15] *Ṣaḥīḥ al-Bukhārī* [Eng. Trans. 1/19 no. 12], *Ṣaḥīḥ Muslim* [Eng. Trans. 1/31 no. 72, 73].

وَإِنَّ مِنكُمْ لَمَن لَّيُبَطِّئَنَّ
فَإِنْ أَصَٰبَتْكُم مُّصِيبَةٌ قَالَ قَدْ أَنْعَمَ ٱللَّهُ عَلَىَّ إِذْ لَمْ أَكُن مَّعَهُمْ
شَهِيدًا ﴿٧٢﴾ وَلَئِنْ أَصَٰبَكُمْ فَضْلٌ مِّنَ ٱللَّهِ لَيَقُولَنَّ كَأَن
لَّمْ تَكُنۢ بَيْنَكُمْ وَبَيْنَهُۥ مَوَدَّةٌ يَٰلَيْتَنِى كُنتُ مَعَهُمْ فَأَفُوزَ
فَوْزًا عَظِيمًا ﴿٧٣﴾

There is certainly among you he who would linger behind (from fighting in the Way of Allāh). If a misfortune befalls you, he says: 'Indeed Allāh has favoured me in that I was not present among them.' But if a bounty comes to you from Allāh, he would surely say - as if there had never been any ties of affection between you and him - 'Oh! I wish I had been with them; then I would have achieved a great success.'

[*Sūrah an-Nisā'* (4):72-73]

So these people who lingered behind did not love for their brother Muslims what they loved for themselves, rather if the Muslims were afflicted with a calamity, they were overjoyed that it only afflicted them, and if they met with blessings they were not happy for them, rather they wished that they too had a portion of this blessing. So they would not become happy except if they received something of this world or some evil of this world was diverted from them. This was due to them not loving Allāh and His Messenger and the Home of the Hereafter, for if this had been the case they would have loved their brothers, and loved what they had received of His blessings and they would have been hurt by the calamity that had afflicted them.

As for the one who is not made happy by what has made the Muslims happy, and is not grieved by what has made the Muslims grieve then he is not of them. In the *Ṣaḥīḥs* of al-Bukhārī and Muslim from ʿĀmir ash-Shaʿbī who said: "I heard an-Nuʿmān bin Bashīr delivering a sermon and saying: I heard the Messenger of Allāh (ﷺ) saying,

> The similitude of the believers with respect to their mutual love, mutual mercy and mutual kindness in like that of one body. When a part of it suffers, the whole body suffers with fever and sleeplessness. [16]

In the *Ṣaḥīḥs* of al-Bukhārī and Muslim from the *ḥadīth* of Abū Mūsā al-Ashʿarī, *raḍiyAllāhu ʿanhu*, who said: "The Messenger of Allāh (ﷺ) said,

> The Muslim to another Muslim is like a building, one part of it strengthens another and he interlaced his fingers. [17]

[2.9 Between Jealousy and Miserliness]

Greed is a sickness as is miserliness, and jealousy is worse than miserliness as occurs in the *ḥadīth* reported by Abū Dāwūd[18]

---

[16] *Ṣaḥīḥ al-Bukhārī* [Eng. Trans. 8/26 no. 40], *Ṣaḥīḥ Muslim* [Eng. Trans. 4/1368 no. 6258].

[17] *Ṣaḥīḥ al-Bukhārī* [Eng. Trans. 8/34 no. 55], *Ṣaḥīḥ Muslim* [Eng. Trans. 4/1368 no. 6257].

[18] This is an error from Ibn Taymiyyah, for the *ḥadīth* in this complete form with this wording is reported by Ibn Mājah [4210]. As for Abū Dāwūd then he

from the Prophet (ﷺ) that he said,

> Jealousy eats away at good deeds, just as fire eats away at firewood, and giving charity extinguishes sins just as water extinguishes fire.

This is because the miser only stops himself from having good but the envier dislikes the favours of Allāh bestowed upon His servants. It is possible that a person give to those lesser than him who would help him achieve his objectives and yet display jealousy to those of the same level as him just as it is possible for him to be miserly without displaying envy to others. Greed is the basis for this as Allāh said,

وَمَن يُوقَ شُحَّ نَفْسِهِۦ فَأُوْلَٰٓئِكَ هُمُ ٱلْمُفْلِحُونَ ﴿٩﴾

> **And whosoever is saved from his greed, such are they who are successful.**
>
> [*Sūrah al-Ḥashr* (59):9]

In the *Ṣaḥīḥs* of al-Bukhārī and Muslim[19] the Prophet (ﷺ) said,

> Beware of greed for it destroyed those that came before you: it commanded them to be miserly and they were, it commanded them to be oppressive and they were and it commanded them to break the ties

---

reports only the first sentence and in the *isnād* of this *ḥadīth* there is an unknown narrator.

[19] This is also an error from Ibn Taymiyyah for this *ḥadīth* has not been reported by al-Bukhārī and Muslim, rather it has been reported by Abū Dāwūd and al-Ḥākim [1/11] and its *isnād* is *ṣaḥīḥ*.

> of kinship and they did. [20]

'Abdur-Raḥmān bin 'Awf[21] used to frequently say in his supplication while make *Ṭawāf*,

> 'O Allāh! Save my soul from greed.' So a person said to him, 'Why is this your most frequent supplication?' He replied, 'When I safeguard myself from greed, I safeguard myself from greed, miserliness and from severing the ties of kinship.'

And jealousy necessarily leads to oppression.

---

[20] *Sunan Abū Dāwūd* [Eng. Trans. 2/445 no. 1694].

[21] As far as I know from what is preserved is that it was Sa'd bin Abī Waqqāṣ.

CHAPTER III

The Disease of Desires and Passionate Love

[3.1 Between Jealousy and Desires]

Miserliness and jealousy are sicknesses that lead to the soul hating that which would benefit it, and its loving that which would harm it. This is why jealousy was mentioned alongside hatred and resentment in the preceding *aḥādīth*. As for the sickness of desire and passionate love then this is the soul loving that which would harm it and coupled with this is its hatred of that which would benefit it.

Passionate love is a psychological sickness, and when its effects become noticeable on the body, it becomes a sickness that afflicts the mind also. Either by afflicting the mind by the likes of melancholy, or afflicting the body through weakness and emaciation. But the purpose here is to discuss its affect on the heart, for passionate love is the fundament that makes the soul covet that which would harm it, similar is the one weak of body who covets that which harms it, and if he is not satiated by that then he is grieved, and if he is satiated then his sickness increases.

[3.2 The Reality of Passionate love (*ishk*)]

The same applies to the heart afflicted with this love, for it is harmed by its connection to the loved, either by seeing, touching, hearing, even think about it. And if he were to curb the love then the heart is hurt and grieved by this, and if he gives in to the desire then the sickness becomes stronger and becomes a means through which the grievance is increased.

In the *ḥādīth* there occurs,

> Indeed Allāh shelters His believing servant from the world just as one of you shelter your sick ones from food and drink (that would harm them). [1]

In the *ḥādīth* concerning the saving of Mūsā reported by Wahb[2], which is recorded by Imām Aḥmad in *az-Zuhd*,

> Allāh says: 'Indeed I drive away My friends from the delights of this world and its opulence and comfort just as the compassionate shepherd drives away his camel from the dangerous grazing lands. And indeed I make them avoid its tranquility and livelihood, just as the compassionate shepherd makes his camel to avoid the resting-places wherein it would be easy prey. This is not because I consider them to be insignificant, but so that they may complete their por-

[1] A similar *ḥādīth* to this reported by al-Bayhaqī and it is a *ḍaʿīf ḥādīth*. (*refer to Fayḍ al-Qadīr*).

[2] Wahb ibn Munabbih is a noble *tābiʿī*, but this *ḥādīth* is reported from him directly to the Prophet (ﷺ) and is not authentic.

> tion of My Kindness in safety and abundance, the delights of the world will not attract him and neither would desires overcome him.'

Therefore the only cure for the sick lies in his removing the sickness by removing this blameworthy love from his heart.

People are divided into two opinions concerning passionate love: One group says that if falls into the category of intentions and wishes, this being the famous opinion. Another groups says that it falls into the category of imagination and fantasies and that it is a corruption of the imagination since it causes one to depict the one who is loved in other than his true reality. This group went on to say:

> And this is why Allāh has not been described with passionate love (*ishk*) and neither that He passionately loves (*ya'shik*) because He is far removed from this, and one cannot be praised who has these corrupt thoughts.

As for the first group, then from them are those who said:

> 'He is described with passionate love (*ishk*) because it is a complete and perfect love and Allāh loves (*yuḥib*).'

And it is reported in the narration of 'Abdul Wāḥid bin Zayḍ that He said,

> 'The servant will always continue to draw closer to me, loving Me and I loving him (*A'shiquhū*).'

This is the saying of some of the Sūfis but the majority do not apply this word to Allāh, because passionate love is a love exceeding the proper bounds, as for the Love of Allāh then it has no end and cannot exceed the proper bounds. Passionate love is to be considered blameworthy without any exceptions, it is not to be praised when it is directed towards the Creator or created because it is a love that exceeds the proper bounds.

This is also true because the word 'passionate love' is only employed with regards to a man loving a woman or child (or vice versa), it is not employed in things such as the love of one's family, property or status, just as it is not employed with regards to the love of the Prophets and the righteous. Commonly, you will find this word being mentioned alongside a forbidden action, such as loving the woman who is not lawful for him, or loving a child joined with the unlawful glance and touch and other such unlawful actions.

As for the love of a man for his wife or slave-girl which leads him out of the folds of justice such that he does unlawful things for her and leaves what is obligatory - as commonly happens - even to the extent that he may oppress his son born of his old wife due to this love of his new wife, or to the extent that he will do things to keep her happy that would harm his religion and worldly life. For example his singling her out for inheritance that she does not deserve, or that he gives her family authority and property that exceeds the limits set by Allāh, or he goes to excesses in spending on her, or he makes unlawful things possible for her which harms his religion and worldly life. This passionate love is forbidden with regards to one who is permissible for him, so how would it be with regards for one who has passionate love for someone who is unlawful or with regards to two men? For this contains a corruption the extent of which none can assess except the Lord of the servants; it is a sickness that corrupts the religion and objectives of the one who possesses it, then it corrupts his intelligence and then his body. Allāh, the Most High, says,

يَٰنِسَآءَ ٱلنَّبِيِّ
لَسْتُنَّ كَأَحَدٍ مِّنَ ٱلنِّسَآءِ ۚ إِنِ ٱتَّقَيْتُنَّ فَلَا تَخْضَعْنَ بِٱلْقَوْلِ
فَيَطْمَعَ ٱلَّذِى فِى قَلْبِهِۦ مَرَضٌ وَقُلْنَ قَوْلًا مَّعْرُوفًا ﴿٣٢﴾

...Then do not be soft in speech, lest in whose heart is a disease should be moved with desire, but speak in an honourable manner.
[*Sūrah Aḥzāb* (33) : 32]

There are some whose hearts contain the disease of desire and whose perceptions are only skin deep. When the object of the desire submits, the sickness is satiated, and this satiation strengthens the desire and pursuit of the object and hence strengthens the sickness. This is in contrast to the one whose objective is not met, for this failure results in removing the satiation that would strengthen the sickness and thereby the desire is weakened as is the love. This is because the person definitely intends that there be action accompanying his desire, for otherwise all his desire would be is just whisperings of the soul, unless there is some speech or looking accompanying this.

As for the one who is afflicted with this passionate love but holds back and is patient, then indeed Allāh will reward him for his *taqwā* as occurs in the *ḥadīth*:

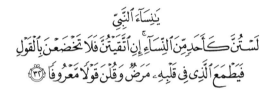

> That the one who passionately loves someone yet holds back, conceals this and is patient, then dies upon this, will be a martyr. [4]

This *ḥadīth* is known to be the report of Yaḥyā al-Qatāt from Mujāhid from Ibn ʿAbbās from the Prophet (ﷺ) but it is problematic and such a *ḥadīth* is not to be depended upon.

But it is known from the evidences of the *Sharīʿah* that if one were to hold back from performing that which is unlawful, be it looking, speaking or acting, and he conceals this and does not articulate it so as not to fall into that which is prohibited and he is patient in his obedience to Allāh and keeping away from disobedience to Allāh, despite the pain that his heart feels due to passionate love, (similar to the case of the one who is patient through a calamity), then indeed this person would gain the same reward as those who have feared Allāh and been patient.

إِنَّهُۥ مَن يَتَّقِ وَيَصْبِرْ فَإِنَّ ٱللَّهَ لَا يُضِيعُ أَجْرَ ٱلْمُحْسِنِينَ ﴿٩٠﴾

> **Verily, he who fears Allāh and is patient, then surely Allāh makes not the reward of the doers of good to be lost.**
>
> [*Sūrah Yusūf* (12) : 90]

This holds true for the disease of envy and all other sick-

[4] A *ḍaʿīf ḥadīth*. Refer to the discussion concerning its inauthenticity in *al-Jawāb al-Kāfī and Rawḍah al-Muḥibbīn* of Ibn al-Qayyim and *Silsilah aḍ-Ḍaʿīfah* of al-Albānī.

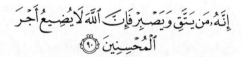

nesses that afflict the heart. So when the soul pursues that which would anger Allāh, and the person prevents himself from this, fearing Allāh, then he is included in His saying,

وَأَمَّا مَنْ خَافَ مَقَامَ رَبِّهِۦ وَنَهَى ٱلنَّفْسَ عَنِ ٱلْهَوَىٰ ﴿٤٠﴾ فَإِنَّ ٱلْجَنَّةَ هِىَ ٱلْمَأْوَىٰ ﴿٤١﴾

But as for him who feared the standing before His Lord, and restrained himself from impure evil desires, and lusts. Verily, Paradise will be his abode.

[*Sūrah Nāz'iāt* (79) : 40-41]

When the soul loves something, it will do all that it can to attain it, so the one who does this out of having a blameworthy love or hatred then this action of his would be sinful. For example his hating a person due to envying him and thereby harming whosoever is linked to that person - either by preventing his rights or by showing them enmity, or his doing something that is commanded by Allāh but he does it due to his desires and not for the sake of Allāh.

These types of sicknesses are commonly found in the heart. The person can hate something and due to this hate, love a great many things due to mere whims and fancies. As one poet affected by this said,

For the sake of a Sudanese girl he loved Sudan to the point
that he loved the black dogs due to his love of her.

So he loved a black girl, and therefore loved all types of black even the blackness of dogs! All of this is a sickness in the heart with regards to its imagination, fantasies and desires. We ask Allāh that He eliminate all of the illnesses from our hearts, and we seek refuge with Allāh from evil manners, desires and sicknesses.

[3.3 The Natural Inclination of the Heart is to love of Allāh]

The heart has only been created for the worship of Allāh, and this is the natural disposition (*fiṭrah*) upon which Allāh created His servants as the Prophet (ﷺ) said,

> Every new-born child is born upon the natural disposition and it is his parents that make him a Jew, Christian or a Magian, as an animal produces a perfect young animal, do you see any part of its body amputated?

Then Abū Hurayrah, (*raḍiyAllāhu ʿanhu*), said, recite if you wish the saying of Allāh,

فِطْرَتَ ٱللَّهِ ٱلَّتِى فَطَرَ ٱلنَّاسَ عَلَيْهَا

> **The *Fiṭrah* of Allāh with which He has created mankind. No change is there in the creation of Allāh.**
>
> [*Sūrah Rūm* (30) : 30][5]

So Allāh has made the natural disposition of His servants to love Him and worship Him Alone, so if the natural disposition

[5] Reported by al-Bukhārī and Muslim.

was to be left as it is without corrupting it, then it would be cognizant of Allāh, loving Him Alone; but the natural disposition does become corrupted due to the sickness of the heart - such as the parents making it a Jew or a Christian - even though this be by the Will and Predecree of Allāh, just like the body is altered by amputation. But even after this it is possible for the heart to return to the natural disposition if Allāh makes this easy for the one who does his utmost to return it to the natural disposition.

The Messengers were sent to affirm and re-establish the natural disposition and to perfect it, not to alter it. So when the heart loves Allāh Alone, making the religion sincerely for Him, it will not be tried by the love of anyone else, not to mention be tried with passionate love because were it to be afflicted with passionate love then this would diminish its loving Allāh alone. This is why when Yūsuf was tried with this passionate love (directed to him) his love of Allāh Alone, making the religion sincerely for him, did not allow him to be overcome by this, rather Allāh said,

لَوْلَآ أَن رَّءَا بُرْهَـٰنَ رَبِّهِۦ ۚ كَذَٰلِكَ لِنَصْرِفَ عَنْهُ ٱلسُّوٓءَ
وَٱلْفَحْشَآءَ ۚ إِنَّهُۥ مِنْ عِبَادِنَا ٱلْمُخْلَصِينَ ﴿٢٤﴾

Thus it was, that We might turn away from him evil and illegal sexual intercourse. Surely he was one of Our chosen, guided slaves.

[*Sūrah Yusūf* (12) : 24]

As for the wife of al-'Azīz, it was because she was and her nation were polytheists that she was afflicted with passionate love. No one, is afflicted with passionate love except that this diminishes his singling out Allāh Alone for worship and his faith. The heart that repents to Allāh, fearing Him, has two routes by which it can remove this passionate love:

[3.4 Preventative Measures from Passionate Love]

1) Repenting to Allāh and loving Him, for indeed this is more satisfying and purer than anything else, and nothing will be left to love along side Allāh.

2) Fearing Allāh, for indeed fear is the opposite of passionate love and removes it.

So everyone who loves something, with passion or otherwise, then this love can be removed by loving that which is more beloved to compete with it.[6]

This love can also be removed by fearing the occurrence of a harm that is more hateful to one than leaving this love. So when Allāh is more beloved to the servant than anything else, and more feared by him than anything else, then he will not fall into passionate love or find any love that would compete with his love of Allāh, except in the case of negligence or at a time when this love and fear has become weak by his leaving some of the obligatory duties and by performing some of the prohibited actions. For indeed faith increases with obedience and decreases with disobedience, so each time a servant obeys Allāh out of love and fear, and leaves a prohibited action out of love and

---

[6] Refer to *Rawḍah al-Muḥibbīn* of Ibn al-Qayyim for he has a beautiful discussion concerning this.

fear, his love and fear becomes stronger, and any love or fear of anything else besides Allāh will disappear from his heart.

[3.5 Some Cures for the Heart]

The same is true for the sickness of the body: for the health of the body is preserved by the same, and the sickness is repressed by the opposite. The correctness of the faith in the heart is preserved by its like, meaning that which would breed faith in the heart from the beneficial knowledge and righteous action for these are its nourishment as occurs in the *ḥadīth* of Ibn Masʿūd, reported as his saying and as a *ḥadīth* of the Messenger (ﷺ),

> Indeed every host loves that people come to his table spread, and indeed the table spread of Allāh is the Qur'ān.

So the Qur'ān is the table spread of Allāh.

From those things that nourish the heart are supplication at the end of the night, the times of *Adhān* and *Iqāmah*, in his prostration, at the ends of the prayers[7] - add to this repentance. For indeed the one who repents to Allāh and then in turn Allāh forgives him, He will then give him enjoyment for an appointed time. That he takes to reciting the reported *adhkār* for the day and at the time he sleeps. That he bears with patience what he is enticed with that would divert him from all of this, for Allāh will immediately aid him with a spirit from Him and write faith

[7] These are the times in which Allāh answers the supplications, there are authentic *aḥādīth* concerning these.

in his heart. That he be eager to complete the obligatory duties such as the five prayers inwardly and outwardly for they are the pillars of the religion. That his words of recourse be

«لَا حَوْلَ وَلَا قُوَّةَ إِلَّا بِاللهِ»

lā hawlā wa lā quwwata illā billāhi[8]

for by them heavy burdens can be born, horrors can be overcome, and the servant be gifted with the best of conditions to live in. That he should not give up the supplication and seeking help from Allāh, for the servant will be answered as long as he is not hasty, saying:

> I have supplicated and supplicated but I have not been answered.[9]

That he should know that help comes with patience, that relief comes after anxiety and distress, that after every period of difficulty there follows a period a period of ease.[10]

That he knows that no prophet or one less than him was rewarded with a good end except as a result of his being patient.

And all praise and thanks are due to Allāh, the Lord of Crea-

---

[8] The Prophet (ﷺ) said, 'indeed it is a treasure from the treasures of paradise.' Reported by al-Bukhārī and Muslim from the *ḥadīth* of Abū Mūsā al-Ash'arī.

[9] Reported by Muslim

[10] A *ḥasan ḥadīth* reported by Aḥmad and at-Tirmidhī from the *ḥadīth* of Ibn 'Abbās

tion. To Him belongs praise and grace for guiding us to Islām and the Sunnah, a praise that would suffice His favours to us outwardly and inwardly, as in required for the nobility of His Face and might of His Magnificence. Abundant Peace and Blessings be upon our master, Muḥammad (ﷺ), and upon his family, Companions, his wives - the mothers of the believers, and all those that follow them in good until the Day of Judgement.

The Biographies

[*The Companions*]

'Ā'ishah: bint Abū Bakr *as-Ṣiddīq*, the Mother of the Believers and most beloved wife of the Prophet (ﷺ). She reported many *aḥādīth* from the Prophet and many Companions and Successors reported from her. She died in the year 58H.

'Abdullāh bin 'Abbās: bin 'Abdul-Muṭṭalib bin Hāshim bin 'Abd Munāf al-Qurashī al Hāshimī, the cousin of the Prophet (ﷺ) and the interpreter of the Qur'ān. He was born three years before the *Hijrah* and was called the 'ocean of knowledge' due to his vast knowledge. He took part in the *Jihād* in North Africa in the year 27H and died in the year 68H.

'Abdullāh bin 'Amr: bin al-'Ās bin Wā'il bin Hāshim bin Su'ayd bin Sa'd bin Sahm as-Sahmī. He and his father were Companions. He was literate and attained permission from the Prophet (ﷺ) to write everything he said. He died in the year 65H.

'Abdullāh Abu Jābir: bin 'Amr bin Ḥazzām bin Tha'labah al-Anṣārī al-Khazrajī as-Sulamī, amongst those who gave the pledge of *'Uqbah*. He witnessed *Badr* and was martyred at *Uḥud*.

---

[1] Most of the biographies are taken from the English translation of *-Furqān bayna Awliyā ur-Raḥmān wa awliyā ash-Shayṭān.* The Decisive Criterion between the Friends of Allāh and the friends of Shayṭān Published by Daar us-Sunnah Publishers 2000.

'Abdullāh bin Mas'ūd: bin Ghāfil bin Ḥabīb al-Hadhlī Abū 'Abdur-Raḥmān. One of the scholars amongst the Companions and he witnessed *Badr* and the following battles. He had many virtues and died in the year 32H.

'Abdullāh bin 'Umar: bin al-Khaṭṭāb al-'Adawī, Abū 'Abdur-Raḥmān, the noble Companion and scholar. He reported many *aḥādīth* from the Messenger (ﷺ) and died in the year 73H.

'Abdur-Raḥmān bin 'Awf: bin 'Awf bin Abd 'Awf bin al-Ḥārith al-Qurashī az-Zuhrī, Abū Muḥammad, one of the ten promised Paradise. He migrated to Abysinnia on both occasions and witnessed every battle with the Prophet (ﷺ). He was very rich and very generous when giving in the Way of Allāh. He died in the year 32H.

Abū Bakr as-Ṣiddīq: 'Abdullāh bin 'Uthmān bin 'Āmir al-Qurashī. The first *Khalīfah* of the Messenger (ﷺ), his companion in the cave, his closest friend and one of the ten promised Paradise. He was the first man to accept Islaam and died in the year 13H.

Abū ad-Dardā': Uwaymir bin Mālik bin Zayd bin Qays al-Khazrajī al-Anṣārī. There is a difference of opinion concerning his name. He accepted Islām on the day of *Badr* and witnessed *Uḥud*. He was from the Legal Jurists and ascetics of the Companions. He died in the year 32H.

Abū Dharr: Jundub bin Junādah al-Ghifārī. He was from amongst the first to accept Islām, it is said that he was the fifth. He was sent back to his people, to call them to Islam and when the Prophet (ﷺ) made *Hijrah*, he too went to Madinah and accompanied the Prophet (ﷺ) in many of his battles. He was well respected for his knowledge and strict asceticism. He died in the year 32H.

Abū Hurayrah: 'Abdur-Raḥmān bin Ṣakhr ad-Dūsī. His name is greatly differed over. He accepted Islām in the year 7H and reported the most *ḥadīth* from the Prophet (ﷺ). He died in the year 59H.

Abū Mūsā al-Ash'arī: 'Abdullāh bin Qays bin Salīm. He had a beautiful recitation and was one of the scholars amongst the Companions. He died in the year 42H or 44H.

'Alī bin Abī Ṭālib: bin 'Abdul-Muṭṭalib bin Hāshim al-Qurashī al-Hāshimī, the fourth Rightly Guided *Khalīfah* and one of ten promised Paradise. He accepted Islām at the age of thirteen and was famous for his chivalry, bravery and knowledge. He married Fāṭimah, the daughter of the Prophet (ﷺ) and was martyred in the year 40H.

'Anas bin Mālik: bin an-Naḍar bin Ḍamḍam al-Anṣārī al-Khazrajī, the servant of the Messenger (ﷺ). He witnessed *Badr* but was not of age to actually participate. He died in the year 93H.

Jābir bin 'Abdullāh: bin 'Amr bin Ḥarrām al-Anṣārī as-Sulamī, he witnessed the second pledge at *'Uqbah* while he was still a child. It is said that he witnessed *Badr* and *Uḥud* and he reported many *aḥādīth* from the Messenger (ﷺ). He died in the year 74H.

Mu'āwiyah: bin Abū Sufyān bin Ṣakhr bin Ḥarb bin Umayyah bin Abd Shams al-Qurashī al-Amawī. He accepted Islām in the year of the Conquest and witnessed *Ḥunain* and *al-Yamāmah*. He was one of the scribes who would write the revelation and died in the year 60H.

Nu'mān bin Bashīr: bin Sa'd al-Anṣārī al-Khazrajī Abū 'Abdullāh . He was a poet and lecturer and died in the year 65H.

Qatādah: ibn an-Nu'mān bin Zayd al-Anṣārī al-Awsī, Abū 'Amr, he witnessed the pledge of *'Uqbah*, *Badr* and every other battle that the Prophet (ﷺ) fought. He died in the year 23H.

Sa'd bin Abī Waqqāṣ: Sa'd bin Mālik bin Ahīb bin 'Abd Munāf al-Qurashī az-Zuhrī Abū Isḥāq bin Abī Waqqāṣ. One of the ten who were promised Paradise and one whose supplications were answered. He was the last of the ten to pass away in the year 55H.

'Umar bin al-Khaṭṭāb: Abū Ḥafs 'Umar bin al-Khaṭṭāb bin Nufayl al-Qurashī al-'Adawī, the second Rightly Guided *Khalīfah* and one of the ten promised Paradise. He accepted Islām five years before the *Hijrah* and his acceptance was a great victory for the Muslims. He witnessed every battle that the Prophet (ﷺ) witnessed. He was martyred in the year 23H.

[*Others*]

Al-Ḥaṣan al-Baṣrī: Al-Ḥasan bin Abū al-Ḥasan al-Anṣārī. He was trustworthy and precise, noble and famous. He was a great scholar and narrated many *aḥādīth*. He died in the year 110H close to the age of ninety.

Ibn Abī Mulaykah: bin ʿAbdullāh bin Judʿān al-Madanī. He met thirty Companions and was trustworthy and precise, a Legal Jurist.

ʿAbdul-Wāḥid bin Zayd: The *shaykh* of the *Ṣufis* at his time, his supplications were answered. He is trustworthy and precise and died in the year 177H.

Abū Dāwūd: Sulaymān bin al-Ashʿath bin Isḥāq bin Bashīr, Abū Dāwūd as-Sijistānī, the *Imām*, *Ḥāfiẓ* and author of the famous *Sunan*. He died in the year 275H.

Aḥmad: bin Muḥammad bin Ḥanbal bin Hilāl ash-Shaybānī, Abū ʿAbdullāh, the *Imām* of the *Sunnah* and author of the famous *Musnad*. He was known for his knowledge of ḥadīth, *fiqh*, and his *taqwā* and asceticism. He died in the year 241H.

Bukhārī: Muḥammad bin Ismaʿil bin Ibrāhīm bin al-Mughirah, Abū ʿAbdullāh. He was born in the year 194H and became one of the *Imāms* of ḥadīth and was nicknamed -the Leader of the Believers in Ḥadīth. He was extremely intelligent and had a remarkable memory. His life was marked by its simplicity and he was known for his asceticism, worship and generosity. He died in the year 256H.

Ibn Ḥibbān: Abū Ḥātim Muḥammad ibn Ḥibbān al-Tamīmī al-Bustī, the *Ḥāfidh*, *Mujtahid* and author of the famous *Ṣaḥīḥ ibn Ḥibbān*. He died in the year 354H.

Ibn Kathīr: 'Imād al-Dīn Ibn Kathīr, was a scholars of *tafsīr*, language, history and *ḥadīth*. He was born in Jandal in a province of Basrah and then moved to Damasus where he died. His works works include the famous commentary of the Qur'ān, entitled *Tafsīr al-Qur'ān al-'Aẓīm*.

Muslim: bin al-Ḥajjāj bin Muslim al-Qushayrī, Abū al-Ḥusain an-Naisābūrī, the *Ḥāfidh* and one of the great *Imāms* of this nation. He is the author of the *Ṣaḥīḥ* which is the most authentic book of *ḥadīth* after Bukhārī. He died in the year 261H.

Shayṭān: Also called *Iblīs*. He is a Jinn and the enemy of mankind, devoted to leading them astray in any way that he can. The word Shayṭān is derived from the verb *shaṭana* which means to be distant, and indeed Shayṭān is distant from all good.

At-Tirmidhī: Muḥammad bin 'Īsā bin Sawrah bin Mūsā bin ad-Ḍaḥḥāk as-Sulamī at-Tirmidhī, the *Imām*, *Ḥāfidh* and the author of the famous *Sunan*. He was trustworthy and precise and one of the students of Bukhārī. He died in the year 279H.

Glossary of Arabic Terms

Āyah: pl. *āyāt*. Sign, miracle, example, lesson, verse.

ʿAbd: pl. *ʿebād*. slave, servant, worshipper.

Abrār: righteous.

Adhān: *fiqh*: the call to prayer.

Barzakh: barrier, obstruction, an isthmus. *fiqh*: a barrier placed between a person who has deceased and this worldly life.

Bidʿah: innovation, *fiqh*: that which is newly introduced into the religion of Allāh.

Ḍaʿīf: weak. A *ḥadīth* that has failed to meet the criteria of authenticity.

Dīn: religion, way of life.

Dhikr: remembrance, *fiqh*: making mention of Allāh.

Duʿā: supplication, invocation.

Farḍ: see ***wājib***.

Fasād: corruption, decay, and invalidity.

Fatwā: *fiqh*: legal ruling.

Fiqh: understanding and comprehension. *fiqh*: of the rulings and legislation of Islām.

Fisq: pl. *fusūq*. Immorality, transgression, wickedness.

Fitnah: pl. *fitan*. Trial, tribulation, civil strife.

Fiṭrah: primordial nature, the harmony between man, creation and Creator.

Ghayb: the Unseen, those matters beyond our senses.

Ghubṭa: envy, referring to the permissible form of envy where the envier wishes to have the same blessings as the envied but without desiring to see them removed from the envied.

This is opposed to *ḥasad*, the blameworthy form of envy where the envier wishes to see the blessings removed from the envied.

Ḥāfidh: pl. *ḥuffādh*. Ḥadīth Master, commonly referred to one who has memorised at least 100 000 *aḥādīth*.

Ḥadīth: pl. *aḥādīth*, speech, report, account. *fiqh*: a narration describing the sayings, actions, character, physical description and tacit approval of the Prophet (ﷺ).

Ḥajj: *fiqh*: pilgrimage, one of the pillars of Islām.

Ḥalāl: released. *fiqh*: permissible.

Ḥanīf: pl. *Ḥunafā*. Upright and Devout. One who leaves the false religions and beliefs for the truth and does not swerve from it. His outward rectitude reflects what is inside him.

Ḥarām: forbidden, sacred, restricted. *fiqh*: unlawful, that which the legally responsible person is rewarded for leaving and sinful for doing.

Ḥasad: see ***Ghubṭa***.

Ḥasan: good. *fiqh*: a ḥadīth that has met the criteria of authenticity to a sufficient level as would allow it to be used as legal proof.

Hawā: base desires.

Ḥudūd: limits, boundaries. *fiqh*: limits ordained by Allāh, prescribed punishments.

Iḥrām: the ceremonial state of making Ḥajj or the Ḥajj garments themselves.

Imām: model, exemplar. *fiqh*: religious leader, one who leads the congregational prayer or leads a community.

Īmān: faith that also comprises a meaning of submission. Its place is the heart, the tongue and the limbs and it increases with obedience and decreases with disobedience.

Ishk: passionate love.

Isnād: chain of narration.

Jāhiliyyah: Pre-Islāmic Ignorance. Technically this refers to the condition of a people before the guidance of Allāh reaches them, or the state of a people that prevents them from accepting the guidance of Allāh.

Janābah: *fiqh*: state of major impurity.

Janāzah: *fiqh*: funeral prayer, funeral procession.

Jihād: striving in the Way of Allāh to make His Word supreme.

Jinn: another creation besides mankind who are invisible to us. They are also subject to the laws of Islām and will be judged in the Hereafter according to how they lived in this life.

Kāfir: a rejecter of faith, disbeliever.

Khalīfah: pl. *khulafā*. Successor, representative. *fiqh*: of the Prophet (ﷺ), head of the Islāmic state. Also called *Amīr al-Mu'minīn* or Leader of the Believers.

Khawf: fear.

Khuṭbah: sermon, lecture. *fiqh*: Friday sermon.

Makrūh: *fiqh*: disliked, reprehensible, that which the legally responsible person is rewarded for leaving but not punished for doing.

Mawḍu': fabricated *ḥadīth*. That *ḥadīth* which is a lie against the Prophet (ﷺ).

Muḥaddith: pl. *muḥaddithūn*. Scholar of Ḥadīth.

Mujtahid: one who performs *ijtihād*. *fiqh*: that level of scholar who can deduce independent verdicts directly from the primary Islaamic sources.

Munāfiq: hypocrite. *fiqh*: one who outwardly displays Islām but inwardly conceals disbelief. This is the worst type of hypocrisy and its possessor is the worst type of disbeliever, there are other lesser types.

Qaḍā: see **qadar**.

Qadar: Allāhs decree of all matters in accordance with His prior knowledge and as dictated by His wisdom.

Qiblah: *fiqh*: direction to which the Muslims pray, towards the *ka'bah*.

Rahbah: dread.

RaḍiyAllāhu 'anhu/'anhā/'anhum/'anhumā: may Allāh be pleased with him/her/them/both of them.

RahimahAllāh/RahimahumAllāh: may Allāh bestow his mercy upon him/them.

Ramaḍān: ninth month of the Islāmic calendar.

Riḍā: contentment and pleasure.

Riyā': an act of worship undertaken by someone to be seen and praised by others and not purely for Allāh.

Ruqyā: recitation used to cure an illness or disease. It can only be done in the Arabic tongue, in words whose meaning is understood, using verses of the Qur'ān or supplications of the Prophet combined with the belief that it is only Allāh who in reality gives the cure.

Sabābah: fervent longing.

Ṣabr: patience, steadfastness.

Ṣaḥīḥ: healthy, sound, authentic, correct. A *ḥadīth* that has met the criteria of authenticity and can be used as a legal proof.

Ṣalāh: *fiqh*: the second pillar of Islām, the prayer.

Salaf: predecessors, commonly employed to refer to the first three generations of Muslims.

Ṣawm: *fiqh*: fasting, one of the pillars of Islām.

Shaghafah: crazed passion.

Shahādah: testification, witness. The declaration that none has the right to be worshipped save Allāh and that Muḥammad (ﷺ) is the Messenger of Allāh.

Shahwā: carnal lusts.

Sharīʿah: divine Islāmic law as ordained by Allāh.

Sharīk: partner, associate.

Shaykh: old man. *fiqh*: learned person, scholar. *ṣufi*: a guide along the spiritual path.

Shayṭān: Satan, Iblīs, a devil.

Shirk: polytheism, associating partners with Allāh in matters that are exclusive to Allāh.

Sunan: a compilation of *aḥādīth*.

Sunnah: habit, customary practice, norm and usage as sanctioned by tradition. *fiqh*: the sayings, commands, prohibitions, actions, and tacit approvals of the Prophet (ﷺ).

Sūrah: chapter of the Qur'ān.

Ṣurah: image, form, face.

Ṭāghut: all that is falsely worshipped besides Allāh.

Tafsīr: elucidation, clarification, explanation. *fiqh*: of the Qur'ān.

Taqwā: fearful awareness of Allāh, pious dedication, being careful not to transgress the bounds set by Allāh.

Tawakkul: trust and absolute reliance.

Tawḥīd: the foundation stone of Islām, the absolute belief in the Oneness of Allāh - His being the sole Creator and Sustainer, His being the only One deserving worship and His being unique with respect to His Names and Attributes.

Ummah: nation, the Muslim nation.

Wuḍū': *fiqh*: ritual ablution.

Zakāh: *fiqh*: one of the pillars of Islām, an obligatory tax levied on a Muslim wealth subject to certain criteria.

Zindīq: heretic, *fiqh*: Ḥanafī - one who does not adhere to a religion; Others - one who is a disbeliever pretending to be a Muslim.

Ẓālim: one who commits *ẓulm*: injustice, harm, transgression

either against Allāh, himself or another creation.
Zuhd: asceticism.

Bibliography

English References

Hasan, Aḥmad, *Sunan Abu Dawud*; sh. Muḥammad Ashraf Publishers and Booksellers, Lahore, Pakistan.

Khan, Muḥammad Muḥsin, and Ḥilālī, Taqi-ud-Dīn, *Interpretation of the Meaning of the Noble Quran in the English Language*; Dar us-Salaam Publication, Riyaḍ, Saudi Arabia.

Khan, Muḥammad Muḥsin, and Ḥilālī, Taqi-ud-Dīn, *The Translations of the Meaning of Sahih al Bukhari* (9 volumes); Kazi Publications, Lahore, Pakistan.

Robson, James, *Mishkat al-Masabih*; sh. Muḥammad Ashraf Publishers and Booksellers, Lahore, Pakistan.

Ṣiddiqi, Abdul Ḥamid, *Sahih Muslim* (4 volumes); Dar al-Arabia, Beirut, Lebanon

Notes

Notes